The Essence
of
His
Presence

The Essence of
of
His
Presence

Lloyd John
OGILVIE

HARVEST HOUSE PUBLISHERS

EUGENE, OREGON

Harvest House Publishers and the author have made every effort to trace the ownership of the publication rights to the material contained herein. In the event of a question arising from the use of such material, we regret any error made and will be pleased to make the necessary correction in future editions of this book.

Cover by Koechel Peterson & Associates, Minneapolis, Minnesota

Cover photo © Photos.com

THE ESSENCE OF HIS PRESENCE
This book includes revised material from *The Magnificent Vision* and other previously published books.
Copyright © 2007 by Lloyd John Ogilvie
Published by Harvest House Publishers
Eugene, Oregon 97402
www.harvesthousepublishers.com

Library of Congress Cataloging-in-Publication Data
Ogilvie, Lloyd John.
    The essence of His presence / Lloyd John Ogilvie.
        p. cm.
    ISBN-13: 978-0-7369-1728-5 (hardcover)
    ISBN-10: 0-7369-1728-4 (hardcover)
    1. God (Christianity)—Meditations. 2. Spirituality. I. Title.
    BT103.O35 2007
    242—dc22

                                                    2007008148

Printed in the United States of America

07 08 09 10 11 12 13 / LB-SK / 10 9 8 7 6 5 4 3 2 1

*My assistant, Sandee Hastings, typed the
manuscript of this book through several revisions.
I deeply appreciate her commitment to Christ,
her dedication to this project, and her care for
the professional details of my ministry.
My wife Doris has been a constant encourager of
the development of this book. Our conversations
and prayer about it have made it a part of our
faith journey together.*

Contents

Living
Supernaturally

Over the years, I've enjoyed sharing a benediction at the conclusion of worship services that I wrote to leave people with a lasting reminder of the essence of the presence of Christ. It was influenced by St. Patrick's blessing. Aptitudes of the Lord are stressed as the basis of five attributes of His character. His omnipotence, omniscience, and omnipresence are spelled out with an emphasis on His presence before, behind, beside, above, and within us. We all share the need to know Christ better in all five of these dynamic dimensions.

Here then is the essence of the Lord's presence He offers us today:

May the omnipotent, omniscient, omnipresent Christ go with you:
before you to show you the way,
behind you to protect you,
beside you to befriend you,

above you to watch over you,
and within you to enable you to live life to the fullest.

I long for nothing less for you, my reader. My hope is that together we can discover and experience how the Lord wants to bless us. He offers to be with us in these five powerful ways. We will consider each dimension in a personal and practical way, based on promises of Christ and illustrations from daily living.

Often we hear the statement, "To whom much is given, of him much is required." It is equally true that, "Of whom much is required, to him much is provided." You and I have been called to live supernaturally, infused with Christ's presence and inspired by His promises.

This book is about what Christ provides for us in the pressures and problems, the delights and difficulties of life. He provides us guidance, protects our back, takes our hand and walks with us, watches over us to help us grow in His grace, and He lives in us to make us like Himself through a transforming character transplant.

Each time I give my benediction it is a reminder of what Christ is able to provide to me also. Repeatedly I'm called back to claim for myself what I so deeply want for others. Writing and compiling this book has been a fresh experience of the essence of His presence. Join me in answering a call to authentic simplicity in receiving Christ, following Christ, and becoming more like Christ.

Years ago, I came across a magnificent statement about the essence of Christ's presence that has been a constant inspiration to me. The author is unknown, but the language is stunning.

Christ is our Way; we walk in Him.

He is our Truth; we embrace Him.

He is our Life; we live in Him.

He is our Lord; we choose Him to rule over us.

He is our Master; we serve Him.

He is our Teacher, instructing us in the way of salvation.

He is our Prophet, pointing out the future.

He is our Priest, having atoned for us.

He is our Advocate, ever living to make intercession for us.

He is our Savior, saving to the uttermost.

He is our Root, we grow from Him.

He is our Bread; we feed upon Him.

He is our Shepherd, leading us into green pastures.

He is our true Vine; we abide in Him.

He is the Water of Life; we slake our thirst from Him.

He is the fairest among ten thousand; we admire Him above all others.

He is "the brightest of the Father's glory, and the express image of His person"; we strive to reflect His likeness.

He is the Upholder of all things; we rest upon Him.

He is our Wisdom; we are guided by Him.

He is our Righteousness; we cast all our imperfections upon Him.

He is our Sanctification; we draw all our power for holy life from Him.

He is our Redemption, redeeming us from all iniquity.

He is our Healer, curing all our diseases.

He is our Friend, relieving us in all our necessities.

He is our Brother, cheering us in our difficulties.

This is the caring and compassionate, powerful and victorious Lord Jesus Christ I pray will go before, behind, beside, above, and within you each day.

This book expresses my deepest convictions about our omnipresent Lord. It contains personal sharing from recent experiences and study. And by request of so many of my readers, I am also sharing some material I've written previously. In both cases, it is a joy to glorify Christ.

Lloyd John Ogilvie

May the
Lord Go
Before You

1

Christ Is Already There

The LORD will go before you...
—Isaiah 52:12

Whenever I look into the faces of people at the conclusion of worship, I am profoundly moved by the privilege of offering a blessing in the benediction. The etymology of benediction is "good word" or "blessing."

I think of the challenges and opportunities into which people will go, and I long to share hope to prepare them to expect and pray for Christ's best for their future. That longing motivates the first phrases of my fivefold benediction: "May the Lord go with you; may He go before you to show the way." What I really want to communicate in this is—don't be afraid of tomorrow; Christ is already there.

Times of difficulty or discord with people drive us to our knees for profound prayer. In communion with Christ we discover three powerful aspects of His nature—His omniscience, omnipresence, and omnipotence. The Lord knows all about us. There is no place we can go where He is not there to meet us and He will supply us with His power. He is Emmanuel, the inescapable Presence of God with us. We cannot flee from Him. He is like Frances Thompson's Hound of Heaven, tracking us until we stop running and accept His sovereignty over us.

Think of the efforts we've all made at times to escape both Christ's judgment and His love. We've all known times, both before and after we became believers, when we thought and acted like people who were seeking to flee from the Lord's seeing and knowing eye.

And yet, the fact that the Lord knows all and is everywhere is the basis of a viable hopefulness for the future. Wherever we go, whomever we meet, the Lord is already there waiting for us. He not only comes to us in times of need and gives us supernatural power for life's difficulties and challenges. *He also goes before us to prepare the way.*

Almost every day, I talk to people who are worried about the future. Their tomorrows are filled with uncertainties. What's going to happen? What will people do? How will problems be resolved? How will the next steps be revealed? These questions put a cloud over our tomorrows and fill our todays with anxiety.

We cannot be free to enjoy life until we discover that the Lord is way out ahead of us preparing opportunities, opening doors, conditioning the thoughts and reactions of people, and arranging His best for us.

Our task is to dare to move forward under His guidance, expectantly anticipating what He has graciously drafted in His building plan for our lives. I find that idea to be both very exciting and a source of deep inner peace. To realize that confidence, we must experience a profound trust in the presence of the prevenient Lord of the future and be gripped with the conviction that Christ knows us better than we know ourselves. We can say with the psalmist,

> *O LORD, You have searched me and known me.*
> *You know my sitting down and my rising up;*
> *You understand my thought afar off.*
> *You comprehend my path and my lying down,*
> *And are acquainted with all my ways.*

—PSALM 139:1-3

Christ Knows It All

The firm conviction of Christ's omniscience, that He knows everything, relieves us of the burden of thinking that we are on our own with the responsibility of developing our lives to the best of our meager abilities. We develop the idea that life is a struggle, in which prayer is an effort to get Christ's attention and then convince Him to help us with our needs and opportunities. We think of Him as aloof, uninvolved, and One who will help us if we word our prayers correctly and live a life worthy of His concern. He is envisaged as a famous consultant whom we seek to call in to help us.

The other day, a friend of mine and I were talking about a crucial project in which we are involved. The work is a strategic ministry, and its future development is beyond our wisdom. We had decided what we should do but admitted we did not have the skills to pull it off. "What we need to do is call in the best consultant in America to help us," my friend advised. When we agreed on who that was, we wondered if we could get on his schedule, whether we could afford his time, and whether he would consider our needs worthy of his involvement.

Reflecting on that incident, I realized that often we think of Christ in the same way. We forget that He's in charge of our lives, and we are employed by Him rather than He by us! We can't call Christ into our area; He is there before we get there.

He Knows Our Thoughts

Now let's go deeper. Christ knows our thoughts even before we clothe them with words. The fact that He knows our thoughts is a reminder that He can and does help form them. As the author of thought, He engenders the content of our prayers so that we can pray for what He is more ready to give than we may have been to ask.

Knowing that, once again we can join the psalmist—this time in praise.

For there is not a word on my tongue,
But behold, O Lord, You know it altogether.
You have hedged me behind and before,
And laid Your hand upon me.
Such knowledge is too wonderful for me;
It is high, I cannot attain it.

—Psalm 139:4-6

What cannot be attained by human effort is given as a gift of love. The Lord who knows all about us, even our inner thoughts, invades our minds to assure us that He can guide our direction and is there waiting for us when we arrive. The joyous realization of His omniscience can free us to rediscover the powerful truth of His omnipresence—not only where we are now, but where we are going in the future.

He Knows Where We Are

The thought of fleeing Christ turns into an expectation of finding Him in the situations and people ahead of us. We give up the illusions of where we might go where He is not, only to realize He is never absent in any place or circumstance. Such truth does not frighten us as much as it frees us of the fear of the future. The Lord has made us for Himself to love, serve, and glorify Him.

When he accepted that the Lord had gone ahead to prepare his way, he was able to relax and enjoy where he was presently.

What does this mean for you and me? Everything! The Lord has a purpose and plan for each of us, a personal, particularized destiny. He has a will for each of us which is unique and special, envisioned for no one else. His ultimate will for everyone is that we should experience His love and accept our status as His loved ones who are destined to live forever. Within that eternal status, He has a plan for each of us to enjoy the abundant life filled with His presence and power for living out what He has ordained to be His individualized strategy. To help us accomplish that, He guides us in the direction we should go and is always before us to maximize each relationship and opportunity.

I talked to a young executive who was concerned about his future. He was restless to get on with his career. Filled with the normal ambition of a dynamic professional in his late 20s, he wanted to be sure of his next steps. He had not considered that Christ had a plan for him. "How can I find that?" he asked.

We talked about having a converted "wanter." That captured his brilliant mind. Wanting what Christ wanted for him had not been a part of his thinking. Though he was a Christian, he had felt that sorting out his professional plans was his job. Yet when we discussed how much of his time and energy was spent at work, he agreed that Christ would want to help him discover His will for what was actually shaping his values and destiny.

We prayed together that the Lord would guide His wanting and prepare the way before him. Then we talked out what he might want to do with his life as His person. What steps would bring him closer to that life goal? Any new position would have to meet that qualification. When he accepted that the Lord had gone ahead to prepare his way, he was able to relax and enjoy where he was presently. He surrendered his wanting to be an instrument for the revelation of the Lord's will.

A few weeks later, a job opportunity opened up that was tailor-made for him as a perfect next step. To his amazement, he learned that the decision to offer him that position had been made at the very time he was wrestling with his future. The Lord had prepared him for what He had prepared.

In very different circumstances, a woman discovered the same assurance about the prevenient providence of Christ. She faced a seemingly insoluble problem at work. She was deadlocked with a fellow worker in conflict that had resulted in strained communication during the day and anxious, sleepless nights. As a confrontation drew near, she sought me out to talk about what she was to do.

We talked a great deal about the woman who had become her enemy and threatening foe. What had made her the way she was? What were the dynamics causing the competitive conflict between them? Could we dare to believe that Christ wanted reconciliation, the resolution of the conflict, and a mutually affirming friendship between them?

We both agreed that He did. Then I asked, "Do you believe that the same Lord who is here with us is also with this woman, and is preparing her for this forthcoming confrontation?" She had not thought of that. The lines of worry on her face seemed to soften as she considered the possibility.

I said, "The Lord loves this person as much as He does you. He is at work right now breaking down the walls of hostility and resistance. When you meet with her, He will have her ready!" We entered into a time of prayer for her, asking God to change both of them so that His plan for their working relationship could be accomplished.

A few days later, when my friend met with the woman, she found her amazingly receptive. She confided to my friend, "The other day when I was thinking about you and nursing all my grievances about you, suddenly a thought hit me—*Why am I so hard on her? What insecurity is causing me to fear her?* We both have gifts and we ought to help each other."

The Lord had softened her heart. He had opened the way for their reconciliation and engendered the friendship that resulted. He was there before, during, and after the meeting for which my friend had prayed, claiming that the Lord would go before her to prepare the way.

Unless I miss my guess, you too have uncertainties and soul-sized problems clouding your future. I have mine. Then we hear the Lord whisper in our souls, *Come, follow Me into and through what I have planned for you. I'll not allow anything to happen that will not bring you closer to Me and My plans for you. Don't be afraid of the future. I'm already there!*

2

Before You
to Guide You

The Lord goes before us to guide us.
We all urgently need to be sure of that.

The future looms with choices. Some are insignificant and easily made; others are momentous and soul-sized, demanding and difficult. The alternatives are equally beguiling or befuddling. It's difficult to know which bridges to burn and which to cross. A heavy fog of indecision, confusion, and uncertainty gathers around us, and it is dark.

The Midnight Muddle

I call this the midnight muddle of our minds. It is no respecter of persons or timing. It can happen in the brightness of day or the sleeplessness of night. Our minds are darkened. We long for vision of what's best or right. The terrifying possibility of missing the maximum for our lives engulfs us. Suddenly the icy fingers of self-doubt grip our hearts. The intimidating memories of foolish choices and wrong decisions prance about in our minds. The mistakes, misfires, and missed opportunities of years gone by haunt us. The "if onlys" of the past give illegitimate birth to the "what ifs" of imagined dangers. We talk to ourselves about what to do, and we answer ourselves with caution and concern. The midnight muddle becomes a dark night of the soul, and persists through the day.

Crucial Decisions

All of us are on the edge of some crucial decision. The deadline is approaching. Some of us are facing a penetrating evaluation of our next steps. Others have excruciating perplexities which demand difficult decisions. Most of us have people problems in which decisions are painful. And every one of us has daily choices about the investment of time, money, or energy. What shall we do? Career choices, marriage problems, family needs, the passages of life—all dish up more quandaries than we're capable of handling at times.

Focus your mind on a crucial decision you are facing right now. On what basis will you make it? How will you know what you are to do? When you've made the decision, how will you know you've done the right thing regardless of what happens?

It's in the midnight muddle of indecision that we are forced to think about our life agendas and the priorities they dictate.

The reason many people have difficulty with decisions is that they have no game plan for their lives. They drift from crisis to crisis, problem to problem, without a satisfactory value system that works. The exclamation points of happiness become lurking question marks of indecision.

Nine Longing Words

There are nine words which express our longing for guidance. They form life's most crucial question—a question that can turn the midnight muddle into a dawn of vision. It's based on an audacious assumption and a grand assurance—that Christ has a purpose and plan for every individual. If we believe that, we can dare ask, "Lord, what is it You want me to do?"

I have never asked that question without receiving a clear and unambiguous answer. Years of helping people with decisions have convinced me that it is the liberating question when we need to clarify our life agenda, our priorities, and the next steps in the Lord's strategy for us. Our extremity of need for specific guidance always gives the Lord an opportunity to help us evaluate our ultimate direction.

Jesus' Twenty-Three-Word Promise

The answer to the nine words of our question is given in twenty-three words of one of Jesus' most dynamic promises.

Here is a shaft of light for our midnight muddle of uncertainty: "I am the light of the world; he who follows me will not walk in darkness, but will have the light of life" (John 8:12 RSV). The answer to all our questions and the direction for all our decisions is a personal relationship with Jesus Christ Himself.

The Light of the World pierces our darkness, penetrates our minds to show us the way, and helps us assign priorities to the opportunities and challenges which confront us. He is the source of guidance; He gives us the secret of receiving guidance; He provides serendipities of guidance along the way.

Jesus made His dramatic promise in a startling context. I believe it was the final statement of His message on the last night of the Feast of Tabernacles in Jerusalem. People from all over Palestine had come to the Holy City to celebrate the memory of the blessings of God on the Israelites during the wilderness wanderings of the Exodus from Egypt.

God had guided the Israelites with a pillar of cloud during the day and a pillar of fire at night (see Exodus 13:21-22). Moses and the people had obeyed the movement of the pillar. Where it rested they had pitched their tents, and they had moved on only when its movement beckoned them onward. The pillar of fire had been the evidence of the presence of God with them. He had been light in the darkness giving direction and courage; when the pillar had hovered over the tent of Moses, the people had known that God was speaking to them (see Exodus 13:21; 33:9-10).

To commemorate this guidance of God there was a ceremony in the Feast of Tabernacles called the Illumination of the Temple. It was held each night in the Court of the Women. Great galleries were erected around the court to hold the spectators. When the sun had set and darkness settled in the sacred precincts, the people gathered to witness a remarkable spectacle. Four great candelabra stood in the center of the court. At the dramatic moment, these were set ablaze as a memorial to the light God had been to His people in the dark uncertainty of the Exodus. The people would sing and dance with joy and adoration all through the night.

For a moment, imagine yourself in the gallery watching the vivid and impressive ceremony. Let your emotions soar with the people as they celebrate with unfettered delight. Join in singing the psalms of praise for the light in darkness God has given His people in all ages.

Now allow an awesome chill of excitement to run up and down your spine as you watch Jesus walk to the center of the court and stand in the midst of the four candelabra. All eyes turn to Him. His voice pierces above the singing and the rhythm of the tambourines, trumpets, and drums. Pointing to the candelabra, He speaks, and His voice rings like thunder: "I am the light of the world! He who follows Me will not walk in darkness but will have the light of life."

Nothing could have startled and shocked the people any more. It was as if He said, "God's presence was a pillar of fire for Moses and our forefathers. Now the pillar of presence is here in person. I am—*egō eimi!* Yahweh is here to be the light of life. These candelabra will go out by the time the cock crows at dawn, but I am light that lasts and can never be diminished, for I am God's light dispelling the darkness. Come, follow Me, and you will be able to walk in the light forever!"

Jesus' Astonishing Claim

Jesus could not have made a more astonishing claim. The word *light* was directly synonymous with God Himself. The Psalmist asserted, "The LORD is my light and my salvation"; "In Your light we see light"; "Send out Your light and Your truth! Let them lead me" (Psalm 27:1; 36:9; 43:3). Isaiah prophesied, "The LORD will be your everlasting light" (Isaiah 60:19 NIV). Micah's confession of trust was, "When I sit in darkness, the LORD will be a light to me" (Micah 7:8).

In claiming to be the light of the world, Jesus clearly declared Himself as the Messiah. One of the names of the expected Messiah was Light. There could be no question about His self-identification after that!

"Follow Me"

Nor can there be for us. Jesus strides into our midnight muddles with the same awesome claim: "I am the Light of the world, your life. Follow Me!" Discovering our direction, discerning the Lord's will, and making our decisions all begin with living and walking in His light.

In his letter to the early church, John declared the authority of the Light and His central message:

This is the message we have heard from Him and declare to you, that God is light and in Him is no darkness at all…If we walk in the light as He is in the light, we have fellowship with one another, and the blood of Jesus Christ His Son cleanses us from all sin (1 John 1:5,7).

L. Nelson Bell, the physician and missionary father of Ruth Graham, said it plainly: "To be a Christian means to have a vital, personal relationship with Jesus Christ, and until that is established all other concerns are secondary." *Christ Himself is the source of light in our darkness.*

Jesus does for us what light does to the darkness. He illuminates, dispels doubt, and guides. Experiencing the Light is intellectual, emotional, and volitional.

The reason we have difficulties with our decisions and priorities is because of profound intellectual misunderstanding. Our minds are darkened by distortions that debilitate our desire to know and do God's will. We ask, "How can God know and care about me with all the billions of people in the world? What right do I have to seek guidance, knowing what I've been and done? If God knows everything, why pray? If I do pray, how can God answer in a way I can know and understand?" Such questions keep us glued to dead center.

And that's why God came Himself as the Light of the World to penetrate our minds with truth about His nature and His attitude toward us. Jesus told us that God's love is not merited or negated by our goodness or badness. He assured us that He cares about all our needs, that He created us to be able to talk with Him and tell Him about our difficult decisions.

The Light of the World implores us to ask, seek, and knock. He invites us to abide in Him and to open ourselves for Him to abide in us. A divine wisdom can pervade our minds to give us insight, sensitivity, and specific direction. The radiant truth of the pillar of light revealed in Jesus' total message and life is that guidance is the result of an eager mind, honed by habitual communion and conversation with Him.

To See Things As They Are

The cloudy dimness of our minds must be broken through so we can see things as they are—Christ as He is and ourselves as we are. The illumination must be such that at the same time it shows us the truth, it makes it possible for us to deal with it. Jesus, the Light of the World, does exactly that!

The Light of the World not only illuminates our intellectual understanding of truth; He exposes our feelings, attitudes, and hidden sins. Experiencing the Light is an emotional trauma if we are not free. Jesus said,

> This is the judgment, that the light has come into the world, and men loved darkness rather than light, because their deeds were evil. For every one who does evil hates the light, and does not come to the light, lest his deeds should be

exposed. But he who does what is true comes to the light, that it may be clearly seen that his deeds have been wrought in God (John 3:19-21 RSV).

If we wish to be guided by the Light, we must open ourselves to His penetrating truth. Nothing can remain hidden from Him. The darkness of our midnight muddle is often our fear of being known and exposed. We want the Lord to lead us and give us an answer about what we should do. But He resists a simple answer until our emotions have been flooded by His light. He knows we will not be able to act on any guidance He gives until we are at peace with Him and ourselves.

He wants us to live so close to Him that we know intuitively what He would want us to do in a specific situation or relationship.

The Secret of Guidance

The secret of guidance is in following the Light of the World. Guidance is volitional: It is given to those who will to do the Lord's will. He offers us the light of life. The Greek verb translated "to follow" is *akolouthein*. It implies faithfulness, obedience, discipleship, and companionship. Jesus' clarion call was "Follow Me! Walk in My footsteps. Lean on Me. Put Me first in your life." John said, "In Him was life, and the life was the light of men" (John 1:4).

All of our difficult decisions are rooted in clarifying our

priorities on the basis of Jesus Christ's agenda for us. The only way through the darkness is to follow the light He gives us. Any confusion about a specific decision is a telltale sign we need a closer walk with Him. Our times of indecision help us to realize we have lagged behind or taken a path away from Him. We have become too busy for consistent prayer. Then suddenly we are faced with a crisis. Having to seek the Lord's will is a sure sign we've been out of it. The Lord is more than a source of answers for our complexities. He wants us to live so close to Him that we know intuitively what He would want us to do in a specific situation or relationship.

The teaching of the kingdom of God was the central theme of Jesus' teaching. The kingdom means the reign and rule of God in our lives. Jesus came to call into being a new breed of people who would accept His complete and unreserved direction of their lives, who would let His will for them become the guiding priority.

Jesus said He came not to do His own will but the will of His Father. He taught His disciples to pray, "Your kingdom come, your will be done, on earth as it is in heaven" (Matthew 6:10 niv). In the anguish of Gethsemane He prayed, "Not My will, but Yours, be done" (Luke 22:42).

The Key to Knowing the Will of God

Obedience is the key to receiving and knowing the will of

Christ. We are given fresh guidance on the basis of our obedience to previous guidance. When we seek the Light for a dark time of decision-making, and have consistently resisted what we know already, it will be difficult for us to accept the next steps and take them.

"Our wills are ours, we know not how; our wills are ours, to make them Thine." That simple prayer from Tennyson's *In Memoriam* unlocks the Lord's guidance. Jesus promised, "If you continue in my word, you are truly my disciples, and you will know the truth, and the truth will make you free" (John 8:31-32 RSV).

Paul discovered the secret of guidance. His moment-by-moment fellowship with Christ gave him clarity for his daily decisions. He shared the secret with the Christians at Rome.

> I appeal to you therefore, brethren, by the mercies of God, to present your bodies as a living sacrifice, holy and acceptable to God, which is your spiritual worship. Do not be conformed to this world but be transformed by the renewal of your mind, that you may prove [test through experience] what is the will of God, what is good and acceptable and perfect (Romans 12:1-2 RSV).

Paul had learned that, when he committed his life daily in an unreserved surrender, he was given the gift of knowing what the Lord's will was in his choices. The purpose of Paul's ministry to the Gentiles was "to open their eyes, that they may turn from darkness to light" (Acts 26:18 rsv). He challenged people to "cast off the works of darkness and put on the armor of light" (Romans 13:12 rsv).

To Paul, Jesus was the light of God's presence: "It is the God who said, 'Let light shine out of darkness,' who has shone in our hearts to give the light of the knowledge of the glory of God in the face of Christ" (2 Corinthians 4:6 rsv). Christians were "children of light" and "saints of light" for the apostle. He believed that to be in Christ was to be filled with light. The purpose of the Christian life was to walk in the light.

An Incisive Inventory

In that context we can take an incisive inventory based on our ultimate priority of following the Lord. We can ask these basic questions honestly about any course of action:

1. What is my life agenda? My ultimate purpose? Is it to know and do the Lord's will?

2. Which of the alternatives before me will be congruent with this life agenda?

3. Can I do it and keep my priorities straight? Does it contradict any of my basic values?

4. Will it extend the kingdom of God in my own life, relationships, and society?

5. If I made that choice would it glorify my Lord and help me to grow as His person?

6. Would the choice bring me into a deeper relationship with the Lord?

7. Does it enable the ultimate good of all concerned? (The word *ultimate* means that in spite of pain or difficulty, it finally would be creative for everyone involved.)

8. Can I maintain my self-esteem if I make this choice? Can I look back on having done it and still love and accept myself?

9. Will it cause stress, anxiety, or dis-ease of soul?

10. Can I take the Lord with me in every aspect of carrying out the decision?

When I dare to ask and answer these questions, the darkness of the midnight muddle begins to lift. There are alternatives which suddenly seem absurd and untenable. How could I have ever entertained the possibility?

But I must be honest enough to share with you the fact that there have been times when all the alternatives have passed the inventory test. What to do then?

How the Lord Gets Through to Us

That leads to the third aspect of how the Light of the World gives us the light of life. He will use any and all means of getting through to us. If we have surrendered a decision to Him, He begins to marshal all the resources that can help us to be sure of what He wills.

The Bible is basic. When we return to the well of His wisdom in Scripture, He will guide us to passages which deal with people who faced similar decisions, or to verses which flash truth for our complexity.

Recently, I was confronted with the need to give strategic leadership with some people who were facing a perplexing problem. The people involved needed my intervention, but what should I say? Should I be tender or tough? Only the Lord knew what was best. My studies in 1 Thessalonians led me to that dynamic second chapter about how Paul had dealt with the needs of the Thessalonians. He reminded them, "We were gentle among you, like a nurse taking care of her children. So, being affectionately desirous of you, we were ready to share with you not only the gospel of God but also our own selves, because you had become very dear to us" (verses 7-8 RSV). Then I read on, "For you know how," said Paul, "like a father with his children, we exhorted each one of you...to lead a life worthy of God, who calls you into his own kingdom and glory" (verses 11-12). The Lord showed me two dimensions of the leadership that I was to give—firmness, directness, toughness, and yet at the same time tenderness and compassion. As I prayed, I felt the Lord telling me to be both gentle and direct. One without the other would not do. I had my answer.

Often the Lord answers our prayers for guidance through another person. He invades our circumstances with an unexpected gift of grace that makes the next step undeniably clear.

Something said, advice given, or wise counsel communicated can be used by the Lord to drive home to us what He wants us to do.

Be sure of this: The Lord can get through to us! He will use all the resources at His disposal to break through to our minds so that we can understand without any confusion what it is He wants us to do.

But of all the ways the Lord guides us, personal prayer is the ultimate confirmation of His direction. When we have inventoried our lives' agendas and checked our priorities, we must leave the last and final word to Him. He can use our minds and emotions to speak to us. Daily times of prolonged prayer, plus moment-by-moment "flash prayers" prepare us to know what to do.

Solomon gave us a proverbial basis of complete openness to the Lord's guidance. "Trust in the LORD with all your heart, and do not rely on your own insight. In all your ways acknowledge him, and he will make straight your paths" (Proverbs 3:5-6 RSV). The *Living Bible* paraphrase makes that advice all the more impelling. "In everything you do, put God first, and He will direct you and crown your efforts with success."

⚬—⚬ ≖◆≖ ⚬—⚬

The Light of the World goes before us. He is with each of us right now—a pillar of fire in the darkness. God Himself is with us. If we dare to follow Him, we will have the light of life—we will know when to wait and when to move, when to be silent and when to speak.

Speak to Him, thou, for He hears, and spirit with Spirit can meet—
Closer is He than breathing, and nearer than hands and feet.

—Alfred, Lord Tennyson

The Light of the World has ended the midnight muddle. If we ask the Lord for guidance, He will use all means possible to show us the way. We can pray with confidence:

Lord, what is it that You want me to do? I surrender my de-
cisions to You. I believe that if I belong to You totally, You will
show me what to do. Here is my mind, think through it; here
are my emotions, help me feel what is right; here is my will, give
me courage to follow Your priorities for my life. And Lord, now
that I have given this decision over to you, help me not to take
it back with worry in a midnight muddle of fear. Go before me
to show me the way, be my constant Companion, and in Your
presence give me peace. Amen.

3

Before You
to Show You
the Way out
of Loneliness

*May the Lord go with you to show you the way out
of loneliness and home to the heart of the Father.*

Loneliness is more than the absence of people. What comes
to your mind when I say the word *lonely*? What's your image
of loneliness? A derelict on a park bench? A friendless person
away from home in a strange city? Someone separated from
loved ones over the holidays? A person with very few or no
significant, satisfying relationships? A social misfit unable to
relate creatively to others?

Careful. Loneliness is a much more universal emotional
condition than that. We all feel it at times. Some people we'd
least expect to feel lonely are seldom free from the gnawing

pain. It lurks under many a jolly mask, and pulses in the hearts of the most gregarious and outgoing. It's there beneath the busy adequacy or pretended assurance of the popular, the famous, and the attractive people we admire.

One of the most crucial discoveries I have made over the years, working with and listening to people, is that loneliness has little to do with the absence of people. We can feel lonely in a crowd, among friends, in a marriage, in the family, at a sorority or fraternity house, and in a church.

The Anxiety of Unrelatedness

Loneliness is the anxiety of unrelatedness, the disturbing realization of our separateness. It is an aloneness in which we feel an acute, chronic, nondirected sense of alienation. It's when we realize that we are unique, distinct persons with centers of individuality which we long to share, and yet fear exposing, all at the same time. Thomas Wolfe was right: "Loneliness, far from being a rare and curious phenomenon peculiar to myself and a few other solitary men, is the central fact of human existence."

Our profound misunderstanding of loneliness is expressed in the way we admonish ourselves and others when we feel its disquieting pangs. *Get with people,* we say. *Make friends. Get married, change spouses. Join a sensitivity group. Travel. Live a little. Let yourself go. Get rid of your inhibitions. State your needs and demand they be satisfied. Expand your horizons.*

Our flight from loneliness has plunged us into a frantic togetherness. We have clubs for every imaginable purpose and some with no purpose at all. Our time is overloaded with endless activities because we fear having to be alone. We long to have friends; then when we have them, we are alarmed because the feeling of loneliness persists. Singles want to get married to heal their loneliness, only to find out that lack of communication is the nemesis of most marriages.

Celia in T.S. Eliot's *The Cocktail Party* expressed it clearly: "No…it isn't that I want to be alone. But that everyone's alone—or so it seems to me. They make noises, and think they are talking to each other; they make faces, and think they understand each other. And I'm sure they don't."

Not Isolation, but Insulation

Loneliness is not isolation; it's insulation. It's the fear of knowing and being known. A Hollywood star confided to me, "I have agents and bodyguards, a driver to whisk me away after a performance. Then I get home and wonder if I was a success. And my wife and kids don't seem to be impressed that they are living with a star. I have everything I've ever wanted except a truly deep relationship."

A wife shared the pain of not being able to communicate her deepest feelings with her husband. "I wish he really knew me!" she said wistfully. "I feel very lonely." The amazing thing is that, as a leading lady in the Los Angeles social whirl, she receives a lot of recognition.

A teenager said that he found it difficult to talk out his feelings with his parents without their criticism or undue alarm. "They seem so put together, like they never had problems or worries like I have. Sometimes I would just like to talk until I know what I want to say."

A young woman complained that she had developed the conversational habit of saying "Know what I mean?" She feels a need for some response, and now says the pleading words without thinking about it. We all long to register on someone's mind and heart what we're feeling and thinking. Know what I mean?

We can empathize with all these people I've described. I could cite hundreds of others from any one year of serving as a parish pastor or as Chaplain of the U.S. Senate or teaching in a seminary. I am constantly amazed at the loneliness I hear expressed in otherwise adjusted and competent people. It comes out in an unguarded comment, a look in the eye, or undeniable body language. Each of us feels the estrangement and separateness of life. We are individual citadels, walled castles with the moat bridges up most of the time. Who really knows us? Whom do we know deeply? Wistfully we sing, "I've got to walk this lonesome valley. Nobody here can walk it for me. I've got to walk it for myself."

We Do Not Need to Walk Alone

Not so! We do not need to walk it alone. The God who created us has come to walk it with us. In Jesus Christ He comes to heal the essential cause of loneliness. If we define loneliness as the anxiety of unrelatedness, then we can affirm a basic purpose of the incarnation as God's reestablishment of our relationship with Him and one another. He came into a lonely world where people were estranged from Him and one another, and revealed the way of intimacy with Him and others as the cure for loneliness. From Bethlehem to Calvary, God offered love as the antidote for our loneliness.

Loneliness is none other than homesickness for God. It's inbred in us. We cannot escape it. Nothing or no one in this world can fill it. There is in every human being a sublime nostalgia. The Greek root of this word is made up of two parts: *nostos* for "return home," and *algos* for "severe pain." There is a pain of loneliness in all of us to return home. No group, friend, or loved one can fill the longing. They were never meant to. God has placed a longing for Him that no person can satisfy.

> *Lord, Thou art life, though I be dead;*
> *Love's fire Thou art, however cold I be:*
> *No heaven have I, nor place to lay my head,*
> *Nor home, but Thee.*
> —Christina Rossetti

Our Homing Instinct

Our loneliness is a "homing instinct." Just as animals, birds, and fish have a homing instinct capable of leading them back to their original habitats, so we have a loneliness to be at home with God. We've all heard of dogs or cats that have found their way home after being lost at great distances. Pigeons are distinguished for their ability to fly hundreds of miles back to their homes; swallows make an aerial journey of thousands of miles each year and return to the exact nesting place they left. Salmon return to spawn in the very part of the river where they were hatched. The examples from the natural world are many.

God has placed the same instinct in us. And intimate communion with Him is our home. God came Himself to show us the way. That's the impact of Jesus' "I am" declaration: "I am the way...no one comes to the Father except through Me" (John 14:6). Yahweh Himself came and comes in Christ to heal our loneliness.

The Secret of Overcoming Loneliness

It was on the night before Jesus was crucified that He gave the secret for overcoming loneliness. His disciples were feeling the loneliness of impending separation from Him. They feared what was about to happen. Jesus' somber predictions about His death were about to come true. What He said to give the courage is our hope in loneliness.

> Let not your hearts be troubled; believe in God, believe also in me. In my Father's house are many rooms; if it were not so, would I have told you that I go to prepare a place for you? And when I go and prepare a place for you, I will come again and will take you to myself, that where I am you may be also. And you know the way (John 14:1-4 RSV).

What has that to do with loneliness? Everything. Jesus comes from the heart of God to show us the way to the heart of God. That's the secret of healing loneliness, the homesickness for God.

We do not need to be troubled any more. The Greek word translated "be troubled" is *tarassesthō,* which means to be tossed to and fro—like restless waves under the impact of a blast of wind. Jesus' assuring word is ultimately reliable: "Believe in God, believe also in me."

Jesus and the Father are one. Jesus is God's word about Himself—to us. The Father's house is the Father's heart. It's expansive and inclusive. When Jesus said it has many rooms or mansions, He meant that it is our true abiding place. Here the Greek word is *monai,* meaning abiding places. This does not mean that the Father's heart has different abiding places, but an abiding place that is grand and glorious, big enough to include all who come

The Father's heart… is waiting for all the homesick souls who will believe and accept the love and forgiveness offered by God's invitation through His Son.

home through Christ. It is waiting for all the homesick souls who will believe and accept the love and forgiveness offered by God's invitation through His Son.

The Door Is Always Open

Now press on in Jesus' promise. He tells us that the house of God's heart is open not only at our physical deaths, but *now*, as a quality of eternal life to replace our loneliness during our days on earth. Heaven is a condition of relationship which begins now and is absolutely undiminishable by death.

Then Jesus asked, "If it were not so, would I have told you that I go to prepare a place for you?" Where was He going to prepare that place? We usually think of His return to heaven. Not so. I believe He was talking about Calvary. That's where He was going to prepare a place of reconciliation, forgiveness, and acceptance. The verb translated "to prepare" is *hetoimazō*, meaning to make ready. Where else could that be done but on Golgotha?

Welcome Home

It would be after that was completed that the Lord would return in the power of His Spirit. "I will come again, and take you to Myself, that where I am you may be also." According to A.T. Robertson, the literal meaning of the Greek is, "And I shall take you along to My own home."[1] When would that be—when He comes again? I believe He meant not only at the Second Coming, but also after the resurrection and at the present time, when He comes to each of us. Right now!

In that light we can understand how Jesus' "I am" promise of being the Way is the answer to loneliness. He is the way to the heart of God, paved through the sacrifice of Calvary. He takes us by the hand and shows us the way to go home. Until we are "at home" with God now in the days of our lives, we will be lonely. It's inevitable; we were created to dwell in Him, to abide in His heart, and our hearts will be lonely until we come home. And when we do, we are welcomed home as if we never left. An intimate communion of love and forgiveness awaits us. There's only one way to God's heart, the way He ordained—through Jesus Christ, the Way.

The healing of loneliness begins with Christ's leading us home to God's heart. But it does not end there. Christ is not only the way to God, but the way to our true selves. Loneliness is rooted in a complex of factors within us which must be transformed. Christ leads us home to ourselves. Oh, to be at home in our own persons! We cannot develop deep, fulfilling relationships with others until we can live with ourselves. Axel Munthe, the Swedish physician and writer, said, "A man can stand a lot as long as he can stand himself."

Sacred Solitude Overcomes Loneliness

This requires solitude. There is no healing of loneliness without solitude. At the center of our separateness and uniqueness we must dare to see ourselves, to face ourselves, and dare to be ourselves. Jesus taught us the importance of solitude. He retreated periodically to be alone with God and taught His disciples to "come away by yourselves" (Mark 6:31 RSV). The Greek means "come away for yourselves." Come away to allow God to heal, refresh and renew the true person He's created us to be. We must draw into the inner center to allow God to do battle with self-negation and distortion of our self-images. The Lord must show us the way to ourselves before He can be the way to new, satisfying relationships with others.

Solitude is not easy at first. For some it is terrifying. Privacy is not a priority in our present age. Often we escape the need for solitude by flinging ourselves back into conversation with people, into some activity, into some television program, or into hours staring at our computer screen. One man I knew stayed up late each night just to hear the closing devotion on the television, so he could hear a human voice say a benediction and a warm "good night."

But those who dare to persist in a habitual daily time of quiet solitude find resources for living nothing else can provide. It was in the solitude on Patmos when the living Christ laid His hand on John. "And when I saw Him," says John, "I fell at His feet as dead. But He laid His right hand on me, saying to me, 'Do not be afraid; I am the First and the Last. I am He who lives'" (Revelation 1:17-18). Christ lays His hand of blessing and power on us when we are quiet. Then we can ask life's deepest questions and have the Lord raise questions with us about what we are doing with the gift of life.

Here again Jesus has prepared a place—the place of forgiveness, assurance, and hope through the cross. In solitude we can stop running; we can allow Christ to love us. He breaks through the layers of defensiveness and lays us open so that we can see ourselves. His forgiving love reconciles those things in us which cause self-hate and destructiveness. We meet the person in us whom frantic activity and overinvolvement has produced—the depleted self, spent in exhausting human relationships.

Solitude is for incisive listening. There is no creative thinking, no important decision-making, and no change of personality or life style without solitude. As Paul Tillich said, "In the moments of solitude something is done to us. The center of our being, the inner self which is the ground of our aloneness, is elevated to the divine center and taken into it. Therein we can rest without losing ourselves." It's in isolation that the insulation that keeps us from other people is torn away.

What pianist Arthur Rubinstein said of practice, I say of solitude: "If I fail to practice one day, I know it; if I miss practicing two days, my agent knows it; if I refuse to practice three days, my public knows it." And so with us in our relationships. If we have no solitude, we have nothing to give to people when we are with them.

The Way to People

Now Jesus is ready to lead us out of solitude to other people. He is the way of a new humanity. "The Way" became a synonym for Christianity in the first century. The quality of relationships in the early church earned Christians the distinction of being called "followers of the Way." This became the ethics and ethos of the church.

So many of the reasons we are lonely stem from the fact that we do not know how to follow Jesus' way of communication. Here are seven aspects of His way of living with other people which will banish loneliness:

First, Jesus' way is *nondefensive*. It is easy to project onto other people our negative attitudes toward ourselves. Such transference takes place in a subtle manner. When we do not really like and love ourselves, often we expect the same attitude from others. We see other people as possible enemies, and constantly set ourselves up for the disappointment we expected all along. Then an inadvertent, subconscious thing takes place. People feel our insecurity and read back to us in their attitudes what we are feeling about ourselves. And so we continue to be shut up in the prison of loneliness.

A second aspect of Jesus' way is *acceptance*. People long to be with a person who accepts them as they are. Our attitudes toward people are often so filled with our agendas for them that they feel we are trying to control them. We end up feeling lonely because in such a situation people cannot be themselves or open themselves to us, nor we to them.

Third, Jesus' way is *nonjudgmental.* He made it painfully clear that judgmentalism always boomerangs: "Judge not, that you be not judged. For with the judgment you pronounce you will be judged, and the measure you give will be the measure you get" (Matthew 7:1-2 rsv). Judgmental people are lonely people. Not only do others avoid a self-appointed critic, but they are also motivated to return judgment for judgment.

Charles Kingsley, the nineteenth-century English clergy-man and writer, said,

> If you wish to be miserable, you must think about yourself; about what you want, what you like, what respect people ought to pay you, and then to you nothing will be pure. You will spoil everything you touch; you will make sin and misery out of everything God sends you. You can be as wretched as you choose.

As wretched as I choose? Yes! Judgmentalism is the sure path to wretchedness, the loneliness of the self-appointed efficiency expert who tries to check everyone's productivity according to his or her own standards. If we keep that up, we will always be lonely.

Fourth, Jesus' way is the way of *affirmation.* People already know how bad they are; they need to know how great they can become. A warm, sensitive, affirming person will have more friends than he or she knows how to handle. When we follow the way of affirmation, our prisons of loneliness will be invaded by people who want to be with us because of the gracious attitude which we radiate. The world around us waits for someone who will understand, forgive before they ask to be forgiven, and offer comfort for life's failures.

The fifth aspect of Jesus' way is *vulnerability*. This dynamic ingredient means openness about ourselves and a willingness to share both the difficulties and joys of our lives. Ever notice how quickly a friendship grows with a person who shares his or her inner life with us? We feel trusted, affirmed, of value, and free to share ourselves in turn. Honesty with people does not mean telling them what they should do or be, but sharing our own struggles and delights.

Two people come to mind. One has become one of my closest friends. One night while we were having dinner, I shared a very personal hurt in my own life. That moment galvanized our relationship. He has referred to that time repeatedly and has opened his life to me. I could never be lonely with a friend like that.

Another person had real needs and wanted my help. But each time we were together first he had to straighten me out; then he would dump his needs on me, hoping I would respond tenderly and empathically. A love-hate, impulsion-repulsion syndrome was constantly at work beneath the surface. He had never discovered the dynamics of vulnerability—that it was first his to share his needs and ask for help, then to let me share my need and allow him the privilege of giving advice. He was a very lonely man because he treated his friends, wife, and associates the way he did me.

Sixth, Jesus' way is the way of *initiative love.* Most people are so insecure that they will wait to be loved before they are free to love. But when our solitude in the fellowship with Christ has given us the liberating assurance of His love, we can become initiative, first-move lovers of people.

One day, a beautiful young woman came to see Henrietta Mears, the great Christian educator. After spending several hours with that powerful person-liberator, the young woman came out radiant. The young woman later confided that she had gone to see Dr. Mears about her feelings of loneliness, and had confessed that she had few friends. The college student responded, "She asked me to name the qualities I would like in a friend. So I told her I needed people who accepted me, would not misuse me, on whom I could count in spite of everything, and who could share my hopes and dreams. Then Dr. Mears said an amazing thing. 'Go be that kind of friend to other people, and you will find that is what they will be to you.'" Powerful advice about being an initiative lover of people. It's sin to be lonely alone in a lonely world!

Finally, Jesus' way out of loneliness involves *being part of a movement that is following Him in changing the world.* He wants to give us the gift of solitude in which He can transform those things in us which keep us from satisfying relationships with people, and He longs to enable us to be people who conquer loneliness by being wound-healers in others.

＊＋ ≕◆≔ ＋＊

We don't have to be part of the lonely crowd any longer. Jesus walked the lonesome valley for us so we no longer need to walk it alone. Listen to His promise: "Lo, I am with you always." Our response? Well, here is mine.

I cannot do without Thee
I cannot stand alone,
I have no strength or goodness
No wisdom of my own.
But Thou, beloved Savior
Art all in all to me,
And perfect strength in weakness
Is theirs who lean on Thee.

May the Lord go before you to show you the way out of loneliness.

May the Lord
Go Behind You

4

Behind You to Be Your Rear Guard

The God of Israel will be your rear guard.
—Isaiah 52:12

The Lord goes behind us to be our rear guard. We need Him not only to go before us to show the way, but behind us as our rear guard to protect our backs. We need His sure defense against our enemies, against hurting memories, against people, and against Satan himself.

Hurting Memories

Unresolved hurts from the past can sneak up behind us and attack us with stabbing memories of what we have done that causes us remorse or what others have done to us that makes us long for retaliation. I'm amazed by compacted garbage of past slights and oversights we carry inside our highly polished exteriors.

We need the Lord, our rear guard, to step in. "That's enough!" He says as He holds the spears of memory at bay with the shield of His power. "Hold off, you troubling memories!" Then He reminds us of His forgiving love and leads us to His cross.

The ability to remember is a divinely endowed gift. With this endowment we collect knowledge through study and experience. The memory bank in our brains contains all that has happened to and around us, as well as the data and information we have memorized. Our problem is that our facility to remember is not capable of selection. We hold on to good and bad memories with equal tenacity. What shall we do with the troubling memories of what we have done or others have done to us?

The disturbing truth is that we cannot heal ourselves. Rehearsing the troublesome memories often makes them worse than they are. Talking them out with a friend or a trained counselor focuses their debilitating reality, but often does not result in the ability to forget or forgive. The memories that hurt us must be taken to a higher court than our own perception and evaluation. Once we have dredged up the past, we need power greater than our own to deal with what really happened and then receive and mediate healing.

Christ, Healer of Memories

Only Christ, our rear guard, the healing power of the

world, can heal the pain of the past. A crucial aspect of His healing in our lives is the healing of memories. Just as surely as His Spirit at work in our bodies is the source of physical healing, so, too, He can expunge from the tissues of the memory portion of the cerebral cortex the disturbing memories we have surrendered to Him.

The computers of our minds can be cleared of all the memories we harbor of our failures, mistakes, and inadequacies in the past. Those memories, if not forgiven and cleansed, fester in us. Some are so painful they are pressed down into the subconscious, yet signal the conscious mind with disturbing thoughts of guilt, fear, tension, and anxiety. Eventually they congeal into an overall attitude of self-condemnation or dread.

We may believe in Jesus Christ but still carry the heavy burden of hurting memories of our failures and the distressing things people have done or said to us in the past. Only a profound experience of Christ's forgiveness in us, and then through us to others, can set us free. We need to hear and appropriate Christ's words, "Neither do I condemn you." Then we need to say that to ourselves. Finally, we need to say it to people who have hurt us.

Prayer Therapy

One way to appropriate Christ's forgiveness, which I have found very helpful, is through a prayer therapy in the solitude we talked about in the previous chapter. Give yourself the gift of several unencumbered, interruption-free hours. Get off by yourself in comfortable surroundings where you can be quiet.

His healing Spirit will wipe out the anguish, guilt, and judgment you feel toward yourself and the resentment you feel toward others.

Open the time of prayerful reflection by affirming that the Lord is present, that you belong to Him, and that He loves you unreservedly. Think about His atoning death for you. Reflect on His forgiveness, freely offered to you. Repeat these words, "I am forgiven. My confession is not to *be* forgiven, but because I *am already.* I believe it and accept it as a basic fact of my life."

Now take a pen and paper. Ask the Lord to guide your mind to any memories that are distressing you. Let your mind drift freely back over the years. Write out each painful memory carefully. This is your private time with the Lord; don't be afraid to let the memories flow. What causes you to feel guilty, hurt, anxious? Put down both what you've done and what others have done to you. Don't evaluate them yet. Just write what comes to mind.

When the flow of memories subsides, you are ready to go back over the list to pray about each one specifically. Then articulate to the Lord your perception of what you did or what happened to you. Ask the Lord for the forgiveness He's already provided through Calvary. Then thank Him for *your* forgiveness and total absolution. In each case of the memory of your own failure, whatever it was, say your own name and announce to yourself that since Christ does not condemn you, you will no longer condemn yourself. When the memories involve what other people have said or done, picture the person in your mind's eye and say his or her name, along with words of forgiveness.

The Lord will guide the whole process. His healing Spirit will wipe out the anguish, guilt, and judgment you feel toward yourself and the resentment you feel toward others. It can and will happen!

Memories and Physical Health

Our spiritual, emotional, and physical health is dependent on the consistent healing of memories. The memory is part of our thinking brain, in technical terms called the cerebral cortex. It is responsible for our intellectual functions, including thinking, imagining, fantasizing, dreaming, and talking, as well as memory. The cerebral cortex is closely related to the limbic system, which controls our emotions, heartbeat, and breathing as well as the input of hormones into the bloodstream through the hypothalamus, pituitary, and endocrine glands. The limbic system gets its signals from the cerebral cortex.

What we think affects our total nervous system and body functions. When we are troubled, anxious, or under stress, alarm signals are sent, arousing the limbic system's emotional and physiological responses. When we are under inordinate or consistently recurring stress, we keep our system in an agitated state of arousal. One of the results of this is that the limbic system pumps chemicals called catecholamines into the bloodstream. These cause high cholesterol, the overproduction of clotting platelets, and a possible clogging of the veins and arteries. In this highly agitated state, our body's immune system is debilitated, making us more susceptible to disease.

Unhealed memories contribute to a constant state of alarm from the cerebral cortex to the limbic system. The same thoughts are repeated, producing the same response as if the circumstances of the memory were actually happening now. Pile up the bad memories, and our bodies will remain in a state of high anxiety. When we couple memory with the imagination, we actually relive the hurting memory, and our emotions and body responses react accordingly.

Now we can appreciate how crucial the healing of our memories is. Often they must be healed before the body can function properly to ward off physical problems. Prayer for physical healing must include the healing of the memory, if the total nervous system is to be a channel of Christ's healing power. Nursing troublesome memories is like taking a constant dose of poison. It is a sign of lack of love for ourselves, a refusal to accept Christ's love and forgiveness.

The Rear Guard Protects Our Backs

The Lord our rear guard also protects us from people who sneak up behind us and manipulate, gossip, or maneuver behind our backs. Some years ago I was pastor of a large church with 62 people on my staff. One day a group of church officers came to me to warn me about one of the men on the staff. "Watch your back!" they said. I found it took a lot of energy constantly to watch out for what he was up to. Finally, I asked the Lord to be my rear guard and protect me. Years after, the man came to me to confess what he had tried to do to scuttle my ship and to explain what had happened to him.

One day while he was reading Ephesians 4:30-32, the Lord intervened and confronted the man with what he was doing. Some words sounded in his soul louder than a blasting megaphone. *Support your boss or leave your job!* the Lord seemed to say. Fortunately, he chose to be supportive. The Lord had stepped in to be my rear guard and protect my back.

The whole incident reminded me again of the power of words to attempt to assassinate people. I was left to wonder if I could be counted on as a rear guard for loved ones and friends. Not without Christ's rear guard example and powers.

Suited Up for Spiritual Warfare

Another vital part of Christ's protective, rear guard presence is to take us to get us suited up with the full armor of

God. He knows what we will face in any day and wants us fully equipped.

We turn to Ephesians chapter 6 for a description of our armor. Paul had experienced personally how Christ suited him up for battle. The apostle used the present passive imperative when he wrote to the Ephesians, "Be strong in the Lord.... And put on the full armor of God" (Ephesians 6:10-11 NIV). The way to be strong was to trust Christ for strength and allow Him to put on us every part of the armor of God. And why? "That you may be able to stand against the wiles of the devil" (verse 11).

Paul wanted the Christians to know that it is not just human nature that causes life's problems and conflicts. He challenged them to face the motivator of selfishness, divisiveness, negative thinking and negative actions. Satan himself.

Satan is delighted when we blame people or groups for divisiveness or debilitating conflict. He wants to remain anonymous so he can continue his diabolical derision undetected. His wiles and scheming are the problem. Paul says—*face the enemy.* But how do we do this?

Paul had observed firsthand the battle armor of the Roman soldiers. He saw how crucial each part was for protection.

Every day we have decisions to make, people to deal with, work to do, and challenges to meet. What's more, we have temptations to face. We need to put on the whole armor early each day before we meet anyone or attempt anything. The wonderful thing about the whole armor is that it protects every part of our being while Christ is our rear guard. Each part of the armor represents aspects of the essence of Christ's presence: truth, righteousness, peace, faith, salvation, and wisdom.

Stand Firm!

First, "Stand therefore, having girded your waist with truth" (Ephesians 6:14).

The belt of a Roman soldier's equipment was placed around his waist. It held his tunic in place. Without the belt, his tunic would flap about, interfering with his free movement and possibly tripping him. The belt also served as a brace for the lumbar region. It gave the soldier a sense of strength and stability. That's why Paul associated the brace of truth with standing.

Truth helps us to stand with strength as well as to take a stand with courage. Paul is talking about all the implications of truth from Christ the Truth. In Christ we have the ultimate truth about God. His grace and power. We know the truth that Christ died for our sins and that we are selected to be saints. We are loved and forgiven. In the commandments found in Jesus' teachings we have the truth spelled out for our daily decisions and living.

What's more, we have Christ's indwelling Spirit to guide us and give us strength to discern and do His will.

Abiding in Christ is the way we become braced with His truth. He constantly brings us back to reality—His truth about God, about us, about how life is to be lived, and about the specifics of what obedience to Him entails.

A friend of mine puts it this way. "Knowing Christ sure takes the guesswork out of living. I don't have to spend my energies thrashing about. The basics are so clear, and if I'll listen in prayer, the specific marching orders are not long in coming. What a great way to live!"

We are called to love the Lord with our minds, to think clearly about His revealed truth, and to live our lives in congruence with it. Daily Bible study kneads into our minds and souls the truth we need for every situation.

Protection Against Insecurity

Next, we are encouraged to "put on the breastplate of righteousness" (Ephesians 6:14).

Closely related to the brace of truth is the breastplate of righteousness. The truth about our righteousness with God by faith in Christ protects us from Satan's scheming efforts to make us insecure. Satan is the author of the lie that we should try to earn our status with God. The lie that he's constantly trying to sell is that if we're good enough we can earn God's love, or if we work harder we'll earn our salvation.

Often we think Satan's influence is limited to ghastly things he tempts us to think or do. No, one of his most effective maneuvers is to encourage self-righteousness. If he can get us into his program of earning our salvation, he has begun to win in his effort to keep us from enjoying grace.

The breastplate covered a Roman soldier's chest and back from neck to waist. The purpose of the breastplate was to protect the heart and lungs from blows or the piercing penetration of an arrow, sword, or lance.

Our spiritual hearts, the zone of our feelings, need no less protection. The intellectual knowledge of our righteousness through Christ plus the gift of faith to accept it has a powerful effect on our emotional stability. The intellectual comprehension of it directly conditions our emotions.

Christ is our righteousness. He covers us with what Isaiah called the "robe of righteousness" (Isaiah 61:10). Having this assurance we are protected from the roller coaster of emotional highs and lows.

Most of all, with the breastplate of righteousness in place, Satan will not be able to influence us with uncertainties about our relationship with Christ or get us off track by pushing us to strive for what is ours already. And with this security we will be motivated to righteous living.

Surefooted Stability

Our feet are next. Paul says, "Shod your feet with the preparation of the gospel of peace" (Ephesians 6:15).

The shoes Paul observed on Roman soldiers were half-boots

called *cilia*. They were made of leather, had open toes, and were tied around the ankles and shins with straps. The soles were thick and heavy and were studded with hobnails.

These shoes had been carefully designed to provide sure-footed stability and to protect the soldier against sharp objects placed in a battlefield. Often an enemy would place in the ground sticks sharpened to dagger points to cripple an advancing legion.

You may wonder what a Roman soldier's shoes have to do with our battle against Satan's influence and particularly how these shoes can be associated with "the preparation of the gospel of peace."

The word meaning "preparation" in Greek is *hetoimasia* and denotes readiness or surefooted foundation. Both shades of meaning probably were in Paul's mind. In the Christian's walk, the unassailable peace of Christ does make us alert and surefooted in the slippery places. It also protects us from the traps and field spears Satan may have put in our way. The main thing Satan wants to do is put us out of commission. He can't do this when we are protected by peace.

Peace is the direct outgrowth of righteousness. The peace of Christ provides the peace of God. It is the profound assurance of our forgiveness and reconciliation with God through the cross. The estrangement and conflict are over. When this peace grips us, we are compelled to share it with others. We wonder if Paul had Isaiah's prophecy in mind, "How beautiful upon the mountains are the feet of him who brings good news, who proclaims peace" (Isaiah 52:7), when he wrote to the Ephesians about their armor. Satan can't harass a person who has peace and whose purpose is to share that peace with others.

Satan's Incendiary Arrows

That's not all. There's further equipment for battle available to us. "Above all, taking the shield of faith with which you will be able to quench all the fiery darts of the wicked one. And take the helmet of salvation" (Ephesians 6:16-17).

The shield Paul is talking about was called a *scutum* in Latin. It was made with linen-covered wood and leather, with iron strips fastened to the top and bottom. Tall and oblong, the shield protected the whole soldier from the enemy. Its construction was designed to withstand incendiary arrows dipped in pitch and lighted before being sent from the archer's bow.

Most of us can readily understand what's meant by "the fiery darts of the wicked one." When our shield of faith is down, we are pierced by flaming arrows that ignite our impatience, anger, or desires. We can flame with indignation, defensiveness, or destructive criticism. Satan's fiery darts can also be sent into our conscience to set a blaze of guilt over unconfessed sins. Other flaming arrows instigate illicit sexual attractions in the mind with all the fiery passions expressed on the picture screen of our fantasies.

How can the shield of faith protect us against these incendiary arrows of Satan? I believe Paul is thinking of the gift of faith that trusts Christ with our needs moment by moment. A fiery dart can set aflame only the kindling of an unsurrendered need. Intimate, personal, ongoing prayer enables us to trust Christ with our concerns. When we see the flaming arrow heading toward us, we can lift our shield and make a fresh commitment to our Lord.

Protection for Our Thinking

The helmet of salvation is closely related to the shield of faith. It protects our brain not only from fiery darts but from destructive blows that Satan inflicts to hammer away at the security, stability, and safety of our salvation. Our thinking is constantly refortified by the special messages Christ gives us. Our helmet guards our thinking against the invasion of thoughts of discouragement. With its protection we can be hopeful thinkers in a world of negative thinkers. Put on your helmet and hold your shield with confidence today.

The Right Word at the Right Time

And now, put out your hand, take a hold of "the sword of the Spirit, which is the word of God" (Ephesians 6:17).

The sword Paul had in mind was a short dagger used in hand-to-hand combat. For close encounters with Satan, we have the power of the Spirit to bring to mind just the right Scripture promise to cut off his attack. The term Paul used for "word" here is *rhema* rather than *logos.* Jesus Christ is the divine *logos,* God's incarnate Word of revelation of Himself. "In the beginning was the Word, and the Word was with God, and the Word was God...And the Word became flesh and dwelt among us" (John 1:1,14). *Rhema,* on the other hand, is used for a word from Christ that is particularly applicable to a specific need. The Scriptures are filled with these propitious promises. When we store them up in our minds, Christ brings just the right one to mind to claim victory over Satan's influence.

For example, when we are exhausted and need strength, the Spirit uses a *rhema* like Isaiah 40:31: "Those who wait on the Lord shall renew their strength; they shall mount up with wings like eagles, they shall run and not be weary, they shall walk and not faint."

Or when Satan plays on our fears, Isaiah 43:1-2 becomes a sword of the Spirit: "Fear not, for I have redeemed you; I have called you by your name; You are Mine. When you pass through the waters, I will be with you; and through the rivers, they shall not overflow you."

Take hold of Jeremiah 33:3 as a sword when you feel boxed in on all sides by what seem to be impossibilities: "Call to Me, and I will answer you, and show you great and mighty things, which you do not know."

Say to Satan, "Stop meddling with Christ's property. I belong to Him...In His name I intend to live free of caution, reserve, timidity, and anxiety!"

When you're discouraged with your own efforts, listen again to Zechariah 4:6: "'Not by might nor by power, but by My Spirit,' says the LORD."

Or when you feel you have to take it all alone, let Christ remind you: "I will never leave you nor forsake you" (Hebrews 13:5), or "Lo, I am with you always" (Matthew 28:20).

And always pray "with all prayer and supplication in the Spirit, being watchful to this end with all perseverance and supplication for all the saints" (Ephesians 6:18).

The treasure chest of words from the Lord or inspired discernment by the Lord seems bottomless. There's a promise for every situation and enough for every day for the rest of our lives.

A Promise for Every Day

Some time ago, I gathered promises for every day of the year. I had them printed and sent them to my friends all over the country. I encouraged them to memorize one a day to enrich their memory bank with hope.

A friend wrote me about the impact of these promises on his life: "I never realized the power of using specific words from the Lord in particular problems. It is as if these Scriptures were spoken just for me. When I claim them in my prayers, I receive courage."

Prayer is the way we put on the whole armor of God in the battle. This takes more than a brief morning prayer and a "Good night, Lord," as we're falling asleep. In fact, it requires conversational prayer under Christ's guidance throughout the day. He guides us hour after hour, and helps us claim a full suit of armor for each situation.

Our great need is for boldness. Paul asked the Christians in Asia Minor to pray that he might be given courage to speak boldly during his imprisonment in Rome, and he knew that they needed boldness as much as he did.

The source of that boldness came from Christ who had defeated Satan at Calvary. Now, one name sends Satan cowering away with trembling and fear. One name alone can expel his influence and defeat his schemes. It is the name of Jesus Christ, our rear guard.

Claim your authority. Hold out the cross and say to Satan, "Stop meddling with Christ's property. I belong to Him. In the name that's above all names, the name of Jesus Christ, you have no power over me in this situation. In His name I intend to live free of caution, reserve, timidity, and anxiety!"

⊷⊷ ≡✦≡ ⊷⊷

Dr. James Stewart, my professor of New Testament Studies at New College, Edinburgh University, taught me the freedom that comes when we depend on Christ as our rear guard. In his teaching and preaching he often used these following paragraphs:

> Can't you see Him—Christ, with the sword of His Spirit, holding the rear of our march, barring the way of our hereditary foes, delivering us from the menace of their onset, defending us from the even worse disaster of desertion? Where would any of us have been today if Christ had not been our rear guard?

> "But," as John Bunyan put it, in one swift, poignant phrase, "not without great danger to Himself—which made me love Him the more."

Then Dr. Stewart would tell the story of Marshal Ney, who served as Napoleon's rear guard.

> There was an hour—a grey, grim, terrible hour—when Napoleon in Russia, finding Moscow burnt before him and his supplies fast running out, faced round westward to begin the long retreat to Paris. He summoned the man he could count on best, the brave, gallant marshal Ney. "I appoint you, my Marshal," he said, "to command the rear guard. You are to keep the Russians back from the main body of my army. You are to be the breakwater between us and the deluge. You are to block their advance at any price, till I extricate my men from this trap of death and get them home to Europe."

> And Marshal Ney promised that he would do it. He drew his troops into line and slowly, grimly, they began to fight

their way back, taking on themselves the full weight of the Russian march of death, enduring indescribable things from wounds and frost and famine. So the terrible days and nights were passed.

And then, it is said one day long afterwards, when some officers were playing cards in their quarters in Paris, the door of the room opened, and there stood before them the most disheveled figure they had ever seen, old and bent and emaciated, his clothing tattered, his hands trembling and lines of terrible suffering carved deep into his features. "Who are you?" they cried, startled. But suddenly, to one of them, there came a flash of recognition. "Why," he exclaimed, springing to his feet, "it's the Marshal! It's Marshal Ney!" And the others rose, and saluted. "Tell us, Marshal," they said, when they had conquered their astonishment, "tell us what we have been wondering—where is the rear guard?" And the bent, broken figure squared his shoulders a moment, and looked them in the face. "Sirs," he said, "I am the rear guard!" And it was a fact. He alone had seen it through.

Who is this who comes with dyed garments red in His apparel, whose visage is marred more than any man, and His form more than the sons of men; this from whose head and hands and feet sorrow and love mingled down? This is the Christ. "*I am* the rear guard," says Jesus.

Take heart through Christ, take heart! The past is God's and the future is God's; and the power of the love of Jesus to hold your spirit strong and steady is really far greater, if you would but believe it, than the power of outward circumstance to violate your peace. Therefore, pilgrim soul, march singing! March with the serenity of Christ possessing you! Past the milestones of the years keep marching—until the long road leads to sunset and evening star and journey's end, and the towers and turrets of the City of God appear beyond the river.[2]

With Christ as our rear guard, we can press on facing the future unafraid.

5

Behind You to Give You a Worry-Free Week

Goodness and mercy shall follow me.
—PSALM 23:6

With Christ as our rear guard, we can have three days without worry each week: yesterday, tomorrow, and today. A worry-free week! Read on…here's the secret.

━━◄►═◄►━━

I have a cherished photograph on the wall of my study in our home. It is a large, 20-by-23-inch brown-tone photo of a shepherd and his faithful sheepdog following a flock of sheep on a rugged road next to a loch in the Scottish Highlands. The picture won an international photographic competition some years ago. It was given to me by the photographer and winner of the contest, a Scots friend who now lives in Houston.

I had spoken at a prayer breakfast there. He presented me his prizewinning photograph as a gift. I was deeply moved.

As I look up from my desk, I am inspired by the dramatic scene. The shepherd dressed in his coarse Highland tweeds and cap is carrying a staff. It is obvious even from his back that he is walking with a very attentive eye on the flock, as if he knows each sheep individually. The whole scene is one of peace, tranquility, and security.

Daily I'm reminded of the Twenty-Third Psalm and gratefully repeat the psalm with an emphasis on the first, fourth, and last verses:

> The LORD is my shepherd; I shall not want…I will fear no evil; for You are with me; Your rod and Your staff, they comfort me…Surely goodness and mercy shall follow me all the days of my life; and I will dwell in the house of the LORD forever.

Surely David had the image of the shepherd following the flock, protecting it from attack from behind. As a shepherd himself, he knew how much the flock needed a rear guard. He also had learned from experience as a leader how much he needed the Lord to protect his back.

The Good Shepherd, Our Rear Guard

And now we have the Good Shepherd, Jesus, to follow us

with His goodness and mercy. He not only goes before us to show the way; He is our rear guard Shepherd.

Sir Harry Lauder, the famous Scots singer, claimed the protecting care of the Good Shepherd at a time of grief. He was in Chicago to sing just after he had lost his son in an untimely death. He prayed that the Lord would help him through the program. After he sang, joy and peace radiated from him to the audience. When he finished, he was given a standing ovation. People would not stop clapping. After he had had numerous curtain calls, Lauder stopped the applause. He said, "Don't thank me; thank the good Lord, the Shepherd of my life, for He put the song in my heart."

We too sing our song because of the protecting care of our Good Shepherd. In this chapter we'll claim David's confidence, "Yea, though I walk through the valley of the shadow of death, I will fear no evil; for You are with me; Your rod and Your staff they comfort me" (verse 4). Then we will renew our trust in Jesus Christ our rear guard, as we reflect on His message in John, chapter 10, about His ministry to help us overcome worry.

The Valley of Shadow

The valley of the shadow of death might be rendered "the glen of deep gloom." David used a familiar Hebrew term here in describing the vicissitudes of walking in a dangerous place, through a difficult experience, or even facing death itself. A portion of that road from Jerusalem to the Dead Sea was called the Valley of the Shadow. Even there, his Shepherd would be with him. The enemies that might attack would be overcome. He had known that in a multitude of battles all through his life. The way he had cared for his sheep as a shepherd boy in Judea was an example for him of the way the Lord, in a so much greater way, would continue to care for him as rear guard.

Protecting Care

The protecting care of the shepherd was symbolized by his rod and staff. The rod was taken from the lower trunk and upper roots of a sapling, including the roundness of where the roots were connected to the trunk. Therefore, at the end of the rod there was a gnarled ball that made the three-to-four-foot rod a powerful weapon. A shepherd learned to throw it with deadly accuracy and could also use it to beat off attackers.

The shepherd's staff had a crook on the end of it. It was used not only to reach out to get hold of a wandering sheep, but to keep the sheep together. Interestingly, a shepherd handled a new lamb by the crook because if he touched it with his hands, the smell of his hands would make the mother reject the lamb. The staff was the instrument of tender care. For David, it meant the Lord's protection and His grace. For us, it is a further sign of the fact that when we are open to His direction,

He guides and surrounds us with protecting care each step of the way, in any period of life that may be filled with fear.

Making It to the Lord's Table

The phrase, "You prepare a table before me in the presence of my enemies" (verse 5), is filled with meaning, not only because of the activities of a shepherd, but also because of the nomadic customs of that time. For the shepherd, the table meant those grazing lands high in the mountains that could be reached only after the snow receded. The shepherd carefully prepared the grazing area. He went before the sheep and on his hands and knees went through the grass, pulling out any of the noxious weeds, briars, or thorny growths that would eventually cause difficulty for the sheep. No effort was spared.

David also knew of the custom that a person could not be attacked while eating in another man's tent. If you could reach a friend's tent—even though your enemies were in hot pursuit—you were safe at his table. The Lord feeds us with His grace and holds off the enemies of life—the enemies of our soul, the things that cause us to be afraid, frustrated, and anxious.

No Cost Too High

"I am the good shepherd. The good shepherd gives His life for the sheep" (John 10:11).

A good shepherd counts no cost too high to protect his

sheep. At no time, regardless of what happens, will he leave the flock. He even, Jesus said, will lay down his own life to protect them. He stands immovably between the sheep and the ravaging wolves.

Catch the impact of that. Picture it in your mind. Jesus stands between us and whatever causes us to worry—physical danger, people who would use or misuse us, a hostile fate that would disturb or destroy us, powers of evil. When the going is tough, Jesus will be there! Imagine each of your worries as separate wolves lurking about, ready to attack. Are they too much for the Good Shepherd to handle? Jesus is God with us. He has all power. His providence is our peace. We will never be alone or bereft again.

A Prescription for Worry

In that context I want to share a prescription for worry. Like some prescriptions it has two parts: something we are to take and something we are to do. It is a companion Scripture to Jesus' "I am" promise about being the Good Shepherd. If I could give you a gift, it would be the freedom to receive and respond to Hebrews 13:5-6:

> He Himself has said, "I will never leave you nor forsake you." So we may boldly say: "The Lord is my helper; I will not fear. What can man do to me?"

Every time we are caught in the bind of worry is a new occasion for an exchange with our Lord. We accept His promise to be with us and we give Him our wearying worry. Consider the immensity of His promise: "I will never fail you nor forsake you." Think about both aspects of that. How could the Lord ever fail us? It would be by leaving us friendless and alone in a dangerous situation. And He claims He never will!

Christ, our Good Shepherd, promises that we shall "go in and out and find pasture" (John 10:9). This is our assurance that all our psychological and physical needs will be met in companionship with Him as He shepherds us. The adventure of the Christian life is not only the assurance of eternal security but the experience of daily security now. Salvation means wholeness, healing, and health. Our Shepherd knows us and calls us.

He Knows Our Name

When Jesus calls us by name to belong to Him, fear of death is past. We are reconciled forever. Nothing can change our elected status. But that's only the beginning. He couples reconciliation with regeneration. The process of growing in His love means that He will penetrate our conscious and subconscious natures. Anything that could debilitate us will be exposed and exorcised. Mental health is the Lord's gift to His loved ones. He loves us just as we are, but He never leaves us that way.

Our Lord really knows us. He understands how anxious we become over having adequate resources in our daily lives. He knows about unpaid bills and low bank balances. He is aware of how we worry about appearance, success, and security. He empathizes with our concern about deadlines and pressure. He sees into our hearts and knows all about our distress over people we love. Life is not easy. Often it is an endless succession of impossible challenges that press us from one crisis to another. We become insecure, wondering if we have what it takes to pull it off.

The only cure for this kind of objective anxiety, focused in real troubles in a very real world, is found in the Lord's admonition: "Seek first the kingdom of God and His righteousness, and all these things shall be added to you. Therefore do not worry about tomorrow, for tomorrow will worry about its own things. Sufficient for the day is its own trouble" (Matthew 6:33-34).

Oswald Chambers has a way of sending straight arrows of truth into my heart. He usually presses me on the adventure beyond where I ever thought I would dare to go. I hope his penetrating words about worry give you the jab they gave me: "Are you looking unto Jesus now, in the immediate matter that is pressing, and receiving from His peace? If so, He will be a gracious benediction of peace in and through you. But if you try to worry it out, you obliterate Him and deserve all you get." Ouch!

⋯⊶ ══✦══ ⊷⋯

We look back to the Good Shepherd. He owns, protects, sacrifices for the sheep. We can have a carefree contentment rather than the soul-twisting, nerve-stretching rack of worry.

Join me in a commitment not to worry for three days this week: yesterday, tomorrow, and today. That makes a worry-free week! And why not? Our rear guard is the Good Shepherd. He goes behind you to protect you.

May the Lord
Go Beside You

6

Beside You in Life's Struggles

They drank of that spiritual Rock that
followed them, and that Rock was Christ.
—1 CORINTHIANS 10:4

The Israelites were blessed during the Exodus with water from the rock that Moses smote at Rephidim and at Kadesh. The rabbis in Paul's day had a legend that water actually followed the Israelites for 40 years. The legend even suggested that a fragment of rock 15 feet high followed the people and provided water. Perhaps Paul alluded to this rabbinical legend and used it in allegorical fashion when he wrote that the spiritual rock that followed was Christ. What is sure is that Paul believed in the pre-existence of Christ. The Logos through whom creation was accomplished and providence was expressed was surely one with the Father and the Holy Spirit in blessing the Exodus. Even more sure is our conviction that

Christ is the water of life, who goes with us providing refreshment for our parched souls in the struggles of life.

Struggles are the stuff of life for most of us. What are yours? I have mine. Few of us consistently feel good about ourselves; we all have times of insecurity and self-doubt, times when we lack self-esteem. Anxiety is a stranger to none of us. Fears and frustrations track us like angry dogs. We've all had periods of discouragement, disappointment, and feeling depressed. Every one of us has memories that haunt and unfulfilled dreams that hurt.

We need love and yet persist in doing unlovable things. Broken relationships, misunderstandings with people, and distorted communication trouble all of us. Stress raps at the door of every heart and is entertained as an unwelcome tenant for what seems to be an endless visit.

Not all our struggles are internal. We all face difficult situations at work or in society. Progress is slow; conflict seems inevitable. Everyone has his or her share of impossible people. We watch the news, read the daily paper, scan the Internet, and our nerves are jangled by what's happening in the asphalt jungle around us. What could we do about things if we tried? A feeling of impotence engulfs us. We wring our hands in powerless frustration.

Christ Helps Us with Our Struggles

But listen to Christ as He speaks about who He is and

what He can do to help us with our struggles. He is the reigning Lord. He comes to you and me to save us from our sins and to free us from our burdens so that we can live the abundant life.

That is what we need to know in our struggles. The Lord—who defeated the demons of despair that deplete us and who vanquished death and all its powers—is alive! Here and now. With you and me at this moment. He has the power to help us turn our struggles into stepping-stones! Listen to Him: "Lo, I am with you always" (Matthew 28:20).

I have known Christ for 58 years. In those years I have never faced a struggle in which Christ and His promises were not the answer. My problem has not been trusting Him with a specific struggle and finding Him inadequate or unresponsive, but rather not trusting Him soon enough. I have spent 50 years as a pastor listening to people and to their struggles. There has never been a need, a sin, a broken relationship, a problem, or an emotional ailment that Christ could not heal or solve.

Answering Four Basic Questions

Allow me to share four basic questions. How we answer them makes all the difference in how we handle life's struggles.

1. Do you believe that Jesus is who He says He is? Is He truly God with you and therefore Lord over all of life's

circumstances, able to marshal all power in heaven and earth to meet your needs?

2. Do you really believe that Jesus performed miracles in the physical, emotional, and spiritual struggles of people?

3. Do you dare to believe that He can and will perform these same miracles in your life? Can He who is creator, sustainer, and innovator of all that happens make things happen in your life?

4. Are you willing to ask Him to be the triumphant Lord in your specific struggles?

I find that most people can say yes to the first two but become uncertain and reluctant about the last two, and I'm convinced the reason is that our idea of what Christ can do today is debilitated by layers of distorted thinking.

> *The Lord who makes things happen wants to move us out of immobility, out of the cycle of strain, stress, and struggle.*

One layer is formed by the idea that we should be able to handle life ourselves without asking for help. The next layer comes from thinking of our Lord more as a judge of our failures than as an enabler who loves us in spite of what we've done or been. A deeper layer is formed by self-depreciation; we think, *How can the Lord care about me when there are millions of people with greater needs?* But by far the thickest and most resistant layer results from thinking of the Lord in impersonal, historical terms.

We live in two worlds—the world of bold beliefs about what He said and did and the world of bland agnosticism about what He can and will do today. We can start turning our struggles into stepping-stones by claiming His promise to be with us. Christ gives His word, "I will never leave you nor forsake you."

Under all the layers inside us is the person we really are, the real you and me, often feeling alone, troubled by life, constantly battling for security and peace. Christ wants to penetrate through those layers to find us right now. He wants to know us as we are and have us love Him as He is: present, powerful, promising new possibilities. The Lord who makes things happen wants to move us out of immobility, out of the cycle of strain, stress, and struggle.

Here's How to Let Christ Do It

First, identify the struggle that represents your deepest need right now. Press deeper to the real cause of the problem. Why are you struggling? What do you do to cause the struggle? What are the basic assumptions on which the struggle is based? What ideas or feelings cause your reactions to what's happening to you?

Second, imagine how Christ would have dealt with someone with this struggle during His earthly ministry. What would He have said? Now hear Him say, "I am the Lord who makes things happen." If you were that person, what would you tell Him about your need and what would you ask Him to do?

Third, affirm the fact that He knows, cares, and has come to you right now. Tell Him all about the struggle. Leave nothing out or hidden. Tell Him that, more than a solution to the struggle, you need Him. Turn the struggle over to Him completely. Leave the results to Him.

Fourth, expectantly anticipate the way He will make the struggle a stepping-stone. Instead of asking, "*How* can I get out of this?" ask "*What* can I get out of this?"—in order to grow, to become stronger, to be more sensitive to others who struggle.

Fifth, praise Him that He can unleash resources, people, and unanticipated potentials to help you which you could never have imagined possible. That's the excitement of the adventure of the Christian life. When we least expect it, Christ breaks through with blessings—perfectly timed, magnificently suited to our needs.

Acceptance of Authority

All through Jesus' ministry, the basic issue was the acceptance of His authority. When He healed the paralytic, He first forgave the man's sins. The leaders of Israel constantly asked, "By what authority are You doing these things? And who gave You this authority to do these things?" (Mark 11:28). He had told them; they were not listening. He had said again and again, "I Am!" His authority, then and now, is because He is the divine Son of God who existed with the Father God since time began.

Christ's authority is that of the creative Logos, the Word of God. He is the "author of life" (Acts 3:15), the uncreated Creator, the verb of God who makes things happen. "In Him dwells all the fullness of the Godhead bodily; and you are complete in Him, who is the head of all principality and power" (Colossians 2:9-10). The fullness Paul affirmed is meant for us in the frustration of our struggles, but only if we accept the Lord's authority to call the shots.

One of the major causes of emotional sickness is the inability to accept and live with authority. We either acquiesce or rebel. Or, what's worse, we give lip service to Christ's authority and still insist on running our own lives. At this very moment, while I write this and you read it, we are all struggling with the central issue of life: Will we yield to our Lord's will and way? Who's going to be in charge? Who is the ultimate Lord of our lives?

Be Specific About Your Struggle

Let's be very specific. Focus on the particular struggle that is frustrating you today. Then look beneath the circumstances to your inner condition. Can you commit the deeper struggle to our Lord? That's the inner secret of turning our struggles into stepping-stones. The Lord knows all about what we're going through and knows what is best for us. He will bring grace and growth out of the pain. The author of life knows what He's doing. Trust Him!

One of the themes of my ministry through the years has been "Turn your struggles into stepping-stones." That's not just a trite alliteration. I really mean it. I believe it can happen. But most of our struggles are in trying to make it on our own. The struggle usually involves a reluctance to entrust our relationships, responsibilities, problems, and potentials to the Lord. It is usually only after a long struggle of self-effort that we cry out, "Lord, help me!" or "I give up!"

Don't get the idea that I'm suggesting sitting around doing nothing, waiting for the Lord to do everything for us. What I am advocating is a willing will that yields all our affairs to Christ's thought-conditioning and will-conforming inspiration.

The testimony of Christians through the ages is that there is a magic moment in their problems when they surrender them to the Lord. Their vision is brightened, their perception of possibilities enlarged, and their insight and strength increased. The Lord has power to release, people to deploy to help us, and doors to open with new solutions that we never dreamed possible.

The Key of the Will

The will is the key. James Jauncy said, "The Lord will not cross the picket line of the will." I believe that's true. But I also believe that He's at work trying to convince us to open the picket line and invite Him into the complexities and concerns we are confronting.

The will is congealed thought refined to the hot metal of desire. The Lord has a divine-sized task ahead with all of us. And if it is true that the will is the servant of the thinking portion of our brains, then the transformation of our presuppositions, values, goals, and beliefs has to be a reformation of those around His mind. That's what maturing in the Christian life is all about.

This is the reason Jesus spent so much time talking about the will. He knew us well. He knew that the will is like a thermostat that, when opened by the warmth of His love, can release the flow of obedient discipleship. He gave us concrete teaching, parables, and a powerful prayer to help us grow in discipleship. The Lord wants to finish what He's begun.

Our biggest struggles are probably the result of His invasion into our minds. He's at work penetrating into our thinking and willing, but always with empathy and sensitivity. He's never over/against us. He is one with us in our needs and wants to help us let go of our willful control so that the floodgates can be opened to the inrush of His immeasurable power.

Norman Rockwell has given us unforgettable paintings which grab our heartstrings and draw us into the frame of the picture. The secret of doing that was taught him by his teacher, Thomas Fogarty. "Step over the frame, Norman," he urged, "over the frame and live in the picture."

Jesus did that in a sublime way. He stepped into the drama of life and taught us how to release our wills.

"On Earth, as It Is in Heaven"

In the Sermon on the Mount, Christ gave us the Magna Carta of the kingdom of God. In it, He also taught us how to pray about our wills. In the Lord's Prayer, perhaps more properly called the Disciple's Prayer, He outlines how His followers can realize the power of prayer. He shows us that prayer for God's kingdom and His will are inseparably linked. The reign and rule of God in our minds, our lives, our relationships, and our society is the focus of praying for the will of God. To ask for God's kingdom to come is a daring prayer. It is to want the full control of His sovereignty in our lives and all our affairs. And He's more ready to give than we are to ask. In fact, the desire is His gift. And so is the freedom to pray, "Your will be done on earth, as it is in heaven."

I've pondered that "as it is in heaven" for many years. What's your picture of heaven? Mine is greatly enriched by John's vision in the book of Revelation. The thing which always impresses me about his inspired glimpses of heaven is that there is a willing community of all the elders, angels, archangels, and cherubim in praise and adoration to the Lord. They are of one mind and spirit about the plan and purpose of the Lord and are participants in His strategy for the culmination of history, the return of Christ, and the final victory.

Adding to that biblical vision is my foretaste of heaven in those times when I've been completely surrendered and open to the will of God. My will seemed to be congruent and consistent with His, and the joy which surged through my being was sublime. Now multiply that with the factor of the glory of the Lord, and you have an inkling of what heaven will be like. The key words of the elders around the throne are "Hallelujah and amen!" Praise God and so be it.

Now back down to earth: back to your life and mine. Our families. Marriages. Singleness. Jobs and the scramble for a living. Difficult people and impossible situations. A long way from heaven, you say! But the distance from where we are to where the Lord is willing to take us is measured by our willingness to pray, "Your will be done on earth, as it is in heaven." Often crises prompt us to pray it. The goal is to make it as natural as breathing and its blessings of strength and courage as expected as tomorrow's sunrise.

The issue is that just as the essential will of the Lord is that we live abundantly and eternally, so too His will for all our relationships and responsibilities is that they be filled with His love and power. The kingdom must reign in us as persons before there's any effectiveness in praying for it in our affairs.

Knowledge About What to Pray

Prayers for the knowledge of what the Lord wills are the powerful prelude to asking that His will be done. That means sincerely asking what He wants us to be and do in the situations which concern us. Often the question helps, "If I loved Christ with all my heart and wanted His best, regardless of the cost to me, what would I do?"

In the same Sermon on the Mount in which we are admonished to pray that God's will be done, we are given some clear promises and clarifications of what are the basics of doing that will. In the Beatitudes, Jesus describes true joyousness or blessedness as confessing our need; feeling grief over what we and others have done with the gift of life; being meek, completely leadable and moldable; desiring rightness with God and His righteousness in all of life; expressing to others the loving-kindness and mercy we've experienced; wanting God, with purity of heart, more than anything or anyone else; and initiating the peace He has established in our hearts between us and others, between the people of our lives, and in the conflicts of the world in which we live. That's enough, for openers, on what the Lord's will surely is in areas where we long for specific guidance.

But Jesus goes on. Being the salt of the earth is also part of God's will. We are meant to bring zest in life's dullness, preservation of the kingdom's goals, savor with spontaneity and sparkle. Consider carefully what it would mean to be light in your home, on the job, or with your friends. We can be sure that the will of the Lord involves being a contagious witness to what He means to us. We also are assigned the task of understanding and communicating the light of His truth in the darkness of distorted values and conflicts in and between people. That's enough to keep us busy the rest of our lives!

The Heart of the Matter

Now Jesus gets down to the heart of the matter. The heart of the issue is obedience to what we know of God's will. Isaiah 29:13 was on Jesus' mind as He confronted the hardness of the hearts of His people: "These people draw near to me with their mouth and honor me with their lips, but their hearts are far from me." But then Isaiah goes on to promise "a marvelous work and a wonder" that shall be done—a prediction of the Messiah's coming. And His message and life were targeted for the transformation of the heart—the mind, emotions, and will.

The Lord went on in the Sermon on the Mount to spell out His fulfillment of the Ten Commandments in calling for a decision of the will to live them in a much more profound way. Here again we see how the Lord emphasized the will. Beliefs had become fragmented from the volitional power of the brain. The last stage in thinking—decision and desire to act—had been omitted. The endowed capacity of the will became immobilized because of lack of positive use. This volitional power actually was used *against* doing God's commandments instead of obeying them.

But because Christ knew that the Spirit of the Lord was upon Him "to proclaim liberty to the captives" (Isaiah 61:1), He pressed on to give guidance to those who had been released by His love to want to hear Him gladly. The Sermon on the Mount makes little sense and seems like a collection of pious sayings until the Spirit gives the liberating gift in the brain to will to trigger into action the auditory nerve and the awesome mechanism of hearing and registering truth. The volitional part of us has the capacity to implement thought, but also to impair the capacity to receive it.

To those given the will to hear, Jesus gave the startling essentials of His way of life for them. They were to go the second mile, turn their cheeks when insulted, love people who were classified as enemies, and give themselves away without concern for recognition.

Prayer in the Secret Place

Prayer was to be conversation with God in the "secret place," not to impress others, but to allow Him to impress

His will on their minds. He would hear and guide them. And the only line in His model prayer which He explained was that we cannot receive forgiveness unless we give it to others.

The prayer of the kingdom people was to ask, seek, and knock. Ask for the Lord's will, seek what that is, and knock with boldness, knowing that the door of opportunity for doing it will be opened.

Worry and anxiety are cut at their taproot by seeking first the kingdom of God and His righteousness. The one concern that heals all lesser concerns is the concern to put God first in our lives.

And then all of this magnificent guidance for living is nailed down by a clear declaration that "not everyone who says to Me, 'Lord, Lord,' shall enter the kingdom of heaven but he who does the will of My Father in heaven." With messianic authority He had just explained the ramifications of that will. Now He called for the final stage in comprehension—the decision of the will to live them.

The parable of the two builders seals the emphasis. One built on sand, the other on rock. The rains, floods, and wind destroyed the first, but the other was immovable. The foolish builder heard but did not will to act; the wise builder heard and willed to implement the truth.

The same is true for you and me. This brief review of the Lord's teaching from the mount in Galilee above the sea spells out so clearly what it means to pray that God's will be done on earth as it is in heaven. It would be a taste of heaven for us and the people around us if we willed to live it. A multitude of questions about doing the will of God are answered. If we started with the Sermon on the Mount and willed to live its demanding challenges, we would be well on the way; secondary questions about specifics would follow naturally.

This was the life conviction of Dr. Henrietta Mears, whom I quoted earlier. She was the distinguished Director of Christian Education for many years at the Hollywood Presbyterian Church. She led thousands of young people to Christ. Her ministry with college students is a benchmark for evangelism among collegians. Hundreds of them became clergy and church leaders. Several significant movements which are impacting the nation today were begun under her influence. The persistent question asked of her by people was how to find God's will for their lives. She was very direct in dispelling the mystery: "Will is the whole man active. I cannot give up my will; I must exercise it. I must will to obey. When God gives a command or a vision of truth, it is never a question of what He will do, but of what we will do. To be successful in God's work is to fall in line and do it His way."

That's quite a challenge! In the light of it, you and I should dare to trust the vision and direction we already have, and then act on it. That's the secret of receiving more guidance. God unfolds more of His will to those who have acted on what He has already revealed. That's what Jesus told the Jews who marveled at His teaching: "How does this Man know letters, having never studied?" The question brought forth another affirmation of the importance of being willing: "If anyone wants to do His will, he shall know concerning the doctrine, whether it is from God or whether I speak on my own authority." The implication for us is that when we want God's will, we shall know as much as we are willing to act on today. More will come when that is done.

The key that unlocks the clarity of His will is surrender. Our need always to be in control is a misuse of our will. It is defensive thought issuing in a tenacious grip on life, people, and situations. But here again, Christ does not attack our imperiousness. Instead, He creates the thought in us that we are at the end of our own resources and ability, and that He is willing to help us. What seems to be a desperate relinquishment is really an unbinding of our volition to allow Him to love us by doing for us what we could not do ourselves. It isn't that the Lord defeats our wills; He sets us free. And in the act of surrender, we win. A bit of heaven happens! We experience the essence of Christ's presence.

7

Beside You
to Set You Free

Make me a captive, Lord,
And then I shall be free.
Force me to render up my sword
And I will conquerer be.
—George Matheson

In this chapter I want to share how Christ goes beside us to set us free. How He dealt with a friend of mine gives us the secret of true and lasting freedom. Here's his real life story.

My friend was on the verge of throwing off his loyalty to Christ. He was an active leader in his church and was chafing under the responsibilities of living the Christian life. Laboring under a distorted idea of freedom, he longed to be released from Christ's challenge to love unselfishly, forgive unqualifiedly, and care sincerely about others. For a brief time, he looked wistfully at the lives of people whose license he mistook for freedom. He was tempted to join those who did what they wanted, with whomever they wanted, without any consideration of the results.

One night he had a dream. The Lord appeared in the dream. He stood at the foot of my friend's bed and said to him,

> *My disciple, I sense you are finding it difficult and restrictive being My follower. I have come to you tonight to release you. You are free to leave Me and follow your own desires. No longer do you need to pray, carry the responsibilities of working in your church, care for people, or give your time and money for the needs of others. I relieve you completely of any further responsibility.*

The man was awestruck in his dream as the Master continued,

> *You have been a beloved disciple, but your heart is no longer with Me. You have a distorted idea of what it means to be free. You think you will be free if you turn your back on your commitment to Me and follow your own desires, plans, and involvements. A loyalty to tradition is all that keeps you among My followers. You have misunderstood My will for you to be rules and regulations which you resist. Because your commitment is not to Me, but the forms of religion, you are fighting the wrong battle for the wrong reasons. I love you so much that I will not keep you against your will. You are released from any obligations of discipleship. You want to be free apart from Me. I give you the chance to discover that is no freedom at all. Now go!*

My friend awoke in a cold sweat. Suddenly he realized how much he loved and needed Christ. Life apart from Him would be no life at all. He cried out a prayer in the darkness of his room, "Lord, don't leave! I do love You! I don't really want to stop being Your disciple. Take me back. I will be Your disciple forever!"

For hours after the dream, the man lay awake reflecting on his almost lifelike encounter with the Master. He knew enough about dreams to know that the conflict in his mind about freedom had invaded his dreams. A tug-of-war within him was more than his conscious mind could handle. His dream had introduced him to a greater loyalty than his desire to break loose of the inherited restrictions under which he had chafed. But he also suspected that Christ had been the initiator of that dream to clarify the real issue. The experience also alarmed him with how much he needed Christ. That night was the beginning of a new relationship with Christ. It became a turning point in his life.

A Tug-of-War Relationship

A dream like that may be uncommon, but the spiritual condition that led to it is not. Many professed Christians live in what might be called a love-resistance, push-pull relationship with the Master. Their attitudes betray an ambivalent inner heart. Like my friend, many misunderstand true freedom.

They resist the rigors of discipleship because they have no liberating companionship with the Savior to give them power to follow Him with joy. At times, we've all wondered what it might be like to cut loose of responsibility, muffle the voice of conscience, and do what we want. Sometimes we act like we don't want the Savior at all.

Many people have settled for a facsimile of Christian freedom: running their own lives while at the same time saying they believe in Christ. That's no freedom at all!

"I wonder where the wonder went?" a man said colorfully. "The people in my church react to the Lord like they were being put upon; like He should be honored that they have decided to be His disciples. They react to the challenges of evangelism and stewardship with ho-hum blandness. Tradition and sameness do terrible things to blight the growth of enthusiasm. I've often thought it would be a good idea to burn the church membership rolls every year just to see how many would want to join again with a real commitment. And I wonder how many of us the Master would want. It might be a good thing if He drummed some of us out of the corps. It would wake others up to the fact that we're acting like we never really wanted to be disciples in the first place."

That man's impatience may sound a bit severe, but it does have a ring of reality. I hear the same urgency expressed by pastors and church leaders across the nation. It is often most intense when leaders try to mobilize authentic New Testament Christianity in their churches and call members to adventuresome giving and living. The central problem of contemporary Christianity in America is exposed. Many people have settled for a facsimile of Christian freedom: running their own lives while at the same time saying they believe in Christ. That's no freedom at all! In fact, it produces a frustration inside us that results in stress and tension rather than peace and joy.

We are really blessed when the Master gives us a choice like my friend had in his dream. It stabs us awake to the fact that we might not really want, need, and desire the Master.

I remember a staff member in a church I served some years ago. He was negative, critical, hostile, and divisive. Nothing was right in the opinion of this cranky young man. One day I called him into my office for a chat. "My friend," I said, "I don't think we qualify to be your church. I don't measure up to be your boss. There may be someone, someplace, who does, and I want to give you the opportunity to go find him." He was astonished. "What do you mean? I want this job. I really want to work for you and with you!" My response was, "You haven't been acting like it." He was so shocked he asked for a second chance to begin acting and talking like a committed member of the team.

Strange, isn't it? The possibility of the loss of something or someone dear to us suddenly awakens us to what it or they mean to us. It happens when a loved one comes near to death and we are forced to think about what life would be without that person.

It happens between friends when conflict threatens our relationship and we picture what it would be to lose the companionship and encouragement we've enjoyed.

Or a parent complains about the demanding responsibilities of raising a child. Is it worth it—all the worry, care, thankless duties? Then the child has an accident and the young life hangs in the balance. And we cry out, as I heard a mother plead prayerfully in an emergency ward of a hospital, "Oh, Lord, give him back to me! I've complained and fretted about him and his teenage behavior. It's not been easy being his mother. All the midnight hours waiting for him to come home...being taken for granted in spite of all I do for him...the difficulty of not being understood...the distress of not knowing what's going on in his head...the lack of communication. Lord, bring them all back. I'll never complain again, if only You let him live!"

The point is clear: What happens to us when we are faced with the possible loss of a human relationship also occurs when we are forced to think about being released from the challenges and responsibilities of our discipleship to Christ.

True Freedom

Thinking about discipleship to Christ has led me to three conclusions about freedom:

1. True freedom begins and is sustained by a liberating bondage expressed in an unreserved commitment to an ultimate purpose.
2. True freedom is expressed when love is the motivation for accomplishing that purpose.
3. True freedom is exercised when all of life is lived in relationship to that ultimate purpose.

These three conditions of true freedom are illustrated in the greatness we admire in outstanding athletes, musicians, and artists. Excellence is achieved only after prolonged practice. Love for an endeavor presses them on through years of perfecting their ability or talent. All other interests and involvements must be secondary to keep their goal focused. When we admire their skill or ability, we are amazed at the ease with which they perform. But that freedom to excel is the result of an unshakable commitment.

The same is true for our freedom in Christ. When our ultimate desire is to know and serve Him as Lord of our lives, all secondary purposes fall into place. Our lives become focused around our basic purpose to serve Him. His love spurs us on to the goal of doing His will and growing in His likeness. No longer are our energies squandered in a multiplicity of entangling commitments. Motivated by love we are released from the need to do anything which would cripple us. We are free because we are committed. And our only question is, How can we bring all of life under His guidance and perfecting power?

The apostle Paul puts all this into clear focus in his message to the Christians at Rome. Roman Christians had been confused about the difference between license and freedom. Some had fallen back into old sins. Their commitment to Christ was being confused by dabbling in behavior that contradicted their central loyalty to Christ. That was not Christian freedom. Paul had to clarify the issue. Note how he did it in Romans 6:15-18:

> What then? Shall we sin because we are not under law but under grace? Certainly not! Do you not know that to whom you present yourselves slaves to obey, you are that one's slaves whom you obey, whether of sin leading to death, or of obedience leading to righteousness? But God be thanked that though you were slaves of sin, yet you obeyed from the heart that form of doctrine to which you were delivered. And having been set free from sin, you became slaves of righteousness.

Paradoxically, faithfulness to one commitment is the secret of true freedom. Freedom is not squandering our creativity and energies in a multiplicity of directions. We are liberated to live powerful lives when our loyalty and devotion is surrendered to a purpose that is big enough to demand all that we have and are. When that purpose commands our allegiance, total attention, and unswerving devotion, we are set free of the beguiling attraction of all lesser goals. We are able to accept or reject any action or relationship in the light of that one grand commitment.

Freedom means having one Master, one controlling conscription to a vision. Everything and everyone who distracts from that goal must be set aside. All that we do in our daily lives must express that purpose. The value of any involvement or investment of time and talent must, in a discernable way, lead toward the accomplishment of this central reason for which we were born—and born again in our conversion. We are free only when we become a bond servant, a slave, of our ideal. We were created in such a way that it is only in this liberating bondage that we are set free.

Slaves of God

Do those words alarm you? Are you prompted to say, "Hold on, Lloyd—that sounds very rigid and restrictive!"? How can bondage set us free? Think what we might miss in focusing our loyalty so exclusively. And what master is sufficient to deserve that kind of commitment?

Paul answers boldly. He calls Christians to be slaves of

righteousness and slaves of God (Romans 6:18,22). The word *slave* has an incarcerating, constricting, limiting sound to our modern ears. How can being a slave set us free? The Greek word translated as *slave* in these verses in both the Revised Standard and the New King James versions is *douloi,* meaning bond servants or simply servants. In verse 18 the verb form *douloō* is used in the aorist passive indicative, *edoulōthēte:* "You *became slaves* of righteousness." Earlier in his letter to the Roman Christians in Romans 1:1, Paul identified himself as a "servant of Christ." The noun is used in the singular, *doulos.* What he meant was that he and the believers to whom he wrote, were unreservedly bonded to one Master, the Lord. We are to obey Him and bring all of life into a right relationship with Him.

In relational theology this is explained as living in the kingdom of right relationships with the Lord, ourselves, others, and the world. That means seeking to know and then to obey the Lord's will in all these relationships. We are to obey the Lord as King of our lives, not our wandering desires for self-satisfaction, nor for any other person as the source of our security. Loyalty to the Lord cannot be divided and given to anything or anyone else.

Being a bond servant of the Lord and righteousness means the same thing. Righteousness is what God is, in and of Himself. The word *righteousness* is a synonym for all the attributes of God, all rolled up into one word. His truth and goodness,

His grace and mercy, His loving-kindness and forgiveness. The word is a cornucopia of meaning for our freedom.

The righteousness of God was revealed in Jesus Christ's life, death, and resurrection for us. Through the Savior we are made right with God. That reconciliation sets us free to desire to live a righteous life. Our righteousness is bringing all of life into agreement with the Lord. It means adjusting the totality of our life to be an expression of His love, His commandments, and His will revealed to us in prayer and reading of the Scriptures. *And the power to do that is given us in a personal relationship with the Savior. We become free when we commit our lives to Christ and invite Him to live in us and to motivate our obedience to His will. Our freedom grows when we dedicate all our intellectual, emotional, volitional, and physical energies to serve Him.*

⊷⊶⊷

That quality of allegiance and loyalty is as foreign to our thinking today as the words *slave* or *bond servant* are to our ears. We live in a time when people are cautious about binding commitments.

The changing attitude to marriage and the family is an example of this. Couples live together unmarried, thinking that if it works out, perhaps they will get married. Recently a radiant couple came to see me for what I thought was premarital counseling. The woman spoke glowingly of their relationship. "We've tried out living together for five years. Now we think it's time to make it official. But we're so leery of commitments. We've talked it over and want to ask you to leave out the 'as long as we both shall live' part of the vow."

The couple wanted a loophole. And so do others who experiment with extramarital relationships or dabble in what's been called "open marriage," where intimacy is shared with others in addition to their mates. "No one person can have all the qualities you need!" one man said in defense of the practice.

We dare not be simplistic about the growing divorce rate, nor insensitive to the pain and anguish it has caused couples and their families. But, in addition to those who reluctantly take that step because there seems to be no way to stay together, there are countless numbers of couples who take divorce lightly as the easy alternative to lasting commitment.

The same lack of steadfastness in our commitments is found today in friendships, our loyalty to our jobs, and our participation in our churches.

So, let's admit it; Paul's call to be bond servants to the Lord and righteousness does run counter to the mood of our contemporary society. That's why many Christians are not free. We find it difficult to make an unreserved commitment to the Lord and to bringing all of life into consistency with His purpose for us.

Being a bond servant of the Lord and righteousness go

hand in hand. We can't have one without the other. Trying to live a righteous life without the Lord's indwelling power ends in futile efforts at self-generated perfectionism or religiosity. Likewise, trying to enjoy a relationship with the Lord without adjusting all of life to His will soon becomes sloppy subjectivism. The Lord says, "Do you really want to be free? Then give Me your absolute commitment and together we'll shape your whole life into a joyous expression of righteousness."

Free Captives

And what is our response? George Matheson worded a liberating one. "Make me a captive, Lord, and then I shall be free. Force me to render up my sword, and then I will conqueror be."

One of the most moving biblical accounts of this deeper level of freedom is what happened to the servant in Exodus 21:1-7. It was the rule in ancient Israel that a Hebrew servant could serve a Hebrew master for only seven years. During the sixth year of his service he was told that in the seventh year he would be released. But if he had come into bondage without a wife, and his master had given him a wife, he could not take with him his wife or any children born during the six years.

The Exodus account focuses on what should happen if a slave chooses not to be released but to stay with his master, wife, and children.

> If the servant plainly says, "I love my master, my wife, and my children; I will not go out free," then his master shall

bring him to the judges. He shall also bring him to the door, or to the doorpost, and his master shall pierce his ear with an awl; and he shall serve him forever.

Picture in your mind's eye the tender drama behind those regulations. Imagine a master and servant who have come to a relationship of mutual respect, friendship, and trust. Because of the master's kindness and the servant's faithful industriousness, a deep companionship forms. The servant has been treated like a brother and in response he has cared for the master's land, cattle, and possessions as if they were his own.

Both the master and the servant dread the ending of the seven years. The master thinks about it reluctantly: *Soon I must release my cherished servant. It will be difficult to tell him, to let him go.* Likewise the servant contemplates the coming eventuality—what for other servants with hard masters is a day of liberation from bondage, he can only think of as a day of excruciating choices. If he chooses to be released he must leave his master, his beloved wife of a few brief years, and his cherished children. Release seems like the real bondage; remaining with his duties pulses with the righteousness of real freedom.

Eventually the day of choice comes. The master comes to his valued servant and says, "My dear friend, you have been more than a servant. We have worked this land as if it belonged to both of us. I've given you full responsibility and in return you've worked diligently for me. Your wife is like a daughter to me, and your children like my own grandchildren.

It breaks my heart to think of you leaving me or them, but according to the law I must give you that opportunity."

The servant's response was filled with passion. "Master, I love you. I love my wife and children. How can I leave you all behind? My duty, my joy, is here. It is not freedom if I go, but a slavery!"

The ceremony of the piercing of the servant's ear with an awl must have been a jubilant celebration. The pain in the lobe of the ear lasted only for a moment, but the scar was a constant reminder that he had chosen to be free to serve his master, love and enjoy his wife, and raise his children.

Our commitment to the Lord must pass through the same turbulent sea of ultimate choice. We are free to leave our Master, but would that be freedom? We are released to throw off the responsibilities of being a bond servant of righteousness, but would that bring us freedom? No, but given the choice, we are introduced to the real person inside us and to what we really want. And we exclaim, "Master, there is no real freedom without You. Serving You and doing Your will is all I want!"

Truly Free People

Truly free people have been confronted with that choice and have made a commitment to serve Christ forever. They are free because of a controlling passion for an ultimate purpose which is grand and demanding enough to call forth all they are. Then all competing, secondary loyalties are marshaled into place to march to the cadences of the Lord's drumbeat. And because we've put Christ first in our lives, we serve Him in our marriages, or singleness, families, jobs, churches, and communities in a much more creative way.

A further illustration of this awesome choice given us by the Master is in John 6:60-69. At the beginning of Jesus'

The choice of freedom is obedience to the Master... True freedom is lost without Him!

ministry, there were thousands who followed Him. His magnetism, healing miracles, and messages of God's love attracted them. But when He began to talk about the cross, true discipleship, and obedience, many departed. John records with stark reality the people's response to the challenges of the Lord. "From that time many of His disciples went back and walked with Him no more."

As Jesus watched the thinning ranks of defecting followers, He turned to the disciples and asked the question, "Do you also want to go away?" Did He see in their eyes the same desire to get out of their discipleship, to go back to their nets, tax table, or personal agendas? I think so. In a way Jesus' question was, "Some of you also are thinking about leaving, aren't you? I release you. I want you to be My followers because you want to be, not because of obligation or compulsion. You may go back to your old life."

Simon Peter spoke for the whole band of disciples. I've often wondered if they talked it over and elected Simon to speak for them. With tears streaming down his face, the disciple sobbed out the response, "Lord, to whom, shall we go? You have the words of eternal life. Also, we have come to believe and know that You are the Christ, the Son of the living God."

There we have it again. The choice of freedom is obedience to the Master. Shall we leave the Master? Where else can we go? True freedom is lost without Him!

＊

And in our quiet contemplation the startling words sound in our own souls. The Master speaks to us: *Finding it difficult to be a Christian? Straining at the reins? Wondering what you'd do if you were not My disciple? You don't have to stay with Me. Only remain if you really want to.* We close our eyes and picture Him, His winsome loving eyes beckoning us to choose true freedom committed unreservedly to Him, motivated by His love. Then we look from His face to His nail-pierced hand. In it is an awl. *Are you ready?* He asks. *Remember it's forever, but also remember that I'll be with you always.*

How will you answer? How will I? The words of the Hebrew servant and the disciples seem mysteriously appropriate. "I cannot leave you, Lord; I love You. Where else can I go? I am free only in You!"

The Lord goes beside us to set us free!

8

Beside You to Give You True Success

I have come that they may have life,
and that they may have it more abundantly.
—John 10:10

Christ goes beside us to share the secret of being free to know ourselves, be ourselves, enjoy ourselves, and express ourselves. This is the center of the truth about what it means to be a liberated person.

Who Are You?

So often we are told, "Just be yourself!" The advice is given as if it were easy to be ourselves. How can you be yourself if you don't really know who you are?

There are so many pressures on us to conform or shape our lives into the molds of society's ideas of success and happiness.

Often we are pulled in many different directions by family, friends, people at work, even fellow Christians. They use powerful manipulative devices to cram us into those molds, such as solicitous affirmation when we acquiesce or withdrawal of approval and love when we get out of line. Some of us give in to the pressure; others of us rebel. Giving in often causes inner anger, and rebellion can lead to eccentric behavior just to prove we won't be controlled.

The theme song of much of our culture is "I've Got to Be Me!" But once we've asserted our right to be ourselves, we're faced with the demanding responsibility of deciding who we are. Actually who we are is a composite of what we think is important, the kind of personality we project, the goals we are determined to achieve, and the values we maintain.

But often the "I've got to be me!" is a whistling-in-the-dark assertion, exposing that we don't know who the "me" is. If we did know, we wouldn't need to protest so vociferously our right to be ourselves. And all too often the concentration on being ourselves leads us away from our potential. We are so busy defending ourselves there's no time or energy left to discover and be who we really are.

A strange mystery of life is that the more we concentrate on realizing ourselves, the less we are the unique persons Christ destined us to be. Meanwhile our freedom is lost fighting off people pressures and defensive self-assertion.

The undeniable truth is that the self is a reflection of the influence of models we admire, personalities we want to emulate, and the picture of ourselves we have projected on the video screen of our imagination. The important question is, Does that picture, painted with the varied colors and shadings of all that has shaped our self-image represent the fully developed self the Lord created us to be?

And so we stand at the crossroads. It is crucial to see the very different destinations of both roads: self-assertion and self-surrender. The destination of self-assertion is achievement of our purposes, plans, professional goals, and personality structure. The other road is the way of self-surrender to the Lord's purposes and plans for us and its destination is the transformation of our personality into His image. The first road ends in self-centeredness, the second in true self-realization.

The reason so many Christians are not free is that they are trying to travel both roads at the same time. Or what's worse, they are determined to get the Lord to help them become what they want to be. Now the words of the song change: "I've got to be me—and Lord, I expect You to give me the strength and courage to pull it off!"

Recently, at a meeting of pastors, the conversation drifted into a discouraging discussion of difficult people whose personality patterns, attitudes, and ways of relating to others were crippling their effectiveness as Christians. The conclusion was, "Well, that's the way things have always been. Their personalities are set in concrete. The chances of them changing are remote."

Is that true? I'm afraid it is—unless they experience Christ's secret of the transformation of personality. They will not be free and they will rob the people around them of their freedom until they discover and live the powerful paradox of being Christ's free person.

❖

Here it is in two challenging dimensions: Either deny yourself or be denied your unique self; either lose your life or you will lose the possibility of all your life was meant to be. Jesus stated the paradox pointedly:

> If anyone desires to come after Me, let him deny himself, and take up his cross daily, and follow Me. For whoever desires to save his life will lose it, but whoever loses his life for My sake will save it. For what profit is it to a man if he gains the whole world, and is himself destroyed or lost? (Luke 9:23-25).

Familiarity with these words from the New Testament can blunt their liberating power. At first Jesus' challenge sounds negative. But on further reflection, we discover that He has given us the profound secret of lasting freedom in *knowing, being, enjoying,* and *expressing* our true selves. Let's consider all four as we open the great treasure of the spiritual and psychological truth Jesus gave to set us free.

Know Yourself

To know yourself is to deny yourself. But how can the denial of self lead to understanding of the self? At the core of the seemingly negative idea is a very positive possibility. Jesus is calling for the denial of a lesser self for the freeing of a greater self. We give up self-interest, self-determination, self-aggrandizement, and self-defensiveness. The goal is not the protection of ourselves but the achievement of a much more creative picture of ourselves.

The denial of self is not the foolish idea of getting rid of self. That can't be done. The self is the container and transmitter of our thoughts, desires, personality, and vision. We can't obliterate self-awareness any more than we can stop breathing. What we can do is open ourselves to Christ's searching and penetrating honesty. When we deny ourselves, we deny our privacy and right to control the development of ourselves. Self-denial is inviting Christ, the surgeon of the soul, to diagnose who we are and perform surgery on our thinking, attitudes, and personality, cutting away all that interferes with us being liberated people.

Then the Lord gives us a new past and a new future. The key is to take up our cross daily and follow Him. Luke alone among the Gospel writers uses the word "daily" indicating the persistent, evolving, ongoing process. Paul exposes the meaning,

I have been crucified with Christ; it is no longer I who live, but Christ lives in me; and the life which I now live in the flesh I live by faith in the Son of God, who loved me and gave Himself for me (Galatians 2:20).

He also said, "I die daily" (1 Corinthians 15:31). To take up our crosses daily is to crucify our self-assertiveness on a daily basis. The death and resurrection cycle is repeated each day as we surrender our lives to the Lord and are raised by His power to new levels of life.

Taking up our cross daily, dying to self each day, is the secret of enjoying freedom in Christ to the fullest every day. If we commit our needs to Him today, He not only releases us from the strain and stress of running our own lives, but He takes care of our tomorrows. Often obedience today makes it possible for Him to bless us with what He has prepared for a future day. That was illustrated vividly in the life of Eric Liddell in the movie *Chariots of Fire.*

At the Paris Olympics in 1924, the Christian athlete denied himself the right to participate in running on Sunday. He held firm beliefs about observing the Lord's Day. He would not contradict his convictions and refused to run the race for which he had spent years of arduous preparation. Later in the week, because of the magnanimity of a friend and the intervention of the Lord in arranging the circumstances, Liddell was given the opportunity to enter another race. In that event he won the gold medal, placing first in the race. What he denied himself one day because of obedience to the Lord was given him on another day. And Liddell gave the Lord the glory for his victory. The same denial of self marked the athlete's life in his subsequent missionary ministry and his stirring witness to Christ in a Japanese concentration camp during World War II.

Becoming the Model of Our Admiration

The death of self-control is the secret of Christ-control. The old self, centered in on its selfish desires, limited goals, and voracious need for success and advancement is progressively replaced with a new self remolded in Christ's image. We become the model of our admiration. If our self-image must be defended at all costs, we will remain the person we are. If, on the other hand, Christ is invited to live in us and given full access to our thinking, willing, and emotional responses, we will become more like Him every day.

Dr. F.B. Meyer described an experience in his life which helps us discover how to do that. When he was a young man he was very irritable. An old man told him a secret of overcoming that proclivity. The man had found freedom from irritability by turning to the Lord the moment he felt it coming on and saying, "Thy sweetness, Lord."

Amy Carmichael comments on Dr. Meyer's discovery in a very helpful way:

Take the opposite of your temptation and look up inwardly, naming the opposite; Untruth—Thy truth, Lord; Unkindness—Thy kindness, Lord; Impatience—Thy patience, Lord; Selfishness—Thy unselfishness, Lord; Roughness—Thy gentleness, Lord; Discourtesy—Thy courtesy, Lord; Resentment, inward heat, fuss—Thy sweetness, Lord, Thy calmness, Thy peacefulness. I think that no one who tries this very simple plan will ever give it up. It takes for granted, of course, that all is yielded—the "I" dethroned.[3]

Responding to the opportunity to follow Christ is to adopt His purposes as our purposes. We discover the joy of serving rather than being served. Focusing on the self shrivels the growth of the self. Centering our attention on Christ and the people He puts in our lives develops the self into a composite of new characteristics: love, forgiveness, compassion, and sacrificial service. Our attitudes change. We are not enervated by constant efforts to defend our turf. We are freed from aggressive competition, jealousy, and envious hostility. We become much less sensitive to what people do to us and far more sensitive to their needs and what the Lord wants to do for them.

To know ourselves requires the eyes of Christ. He sees us both as we are and what we can be by His indwelling power. He gives us the courage to change aspects of the riverbed of self which block the flow of His Spirit in and through us. But then He shows us how we would look, act, react, and perform with our talents multiplied by His gifts of love, wisdom, discernment, daring faith, and courageous vision.

When we seek to know ourselves with self-analysis apart from Christ we end up not really knowing ourselves. Our minds play tricks on us. They block our ruthless honesty where it is needed and positive affirmation where it is required. The self eludes analysis of the self. But the more we know of Christ the more we can deal with what we've been and the more we can dare to be the unique miracle He wants to work in us to produce.

Be Yourself

Jesus goes on to tell us the next part of His secret of personal freedom: *To be yourself, lose yourself.* "Whoever desires to save his life will lose it, but whoever loses his life for My sake will save it." There are two key words for life used in the New Testament. *Psuchē* is used for natural life, the perishing and limited physical existence of a person and transitory affairs, possessions, and relationships. *Zōē* is a nobler word for the quality of spiritual life offered to us in a relationship with the Lord and as recipients of His Spirit in us. The word *psuchē* is used here in Jesus' admonition. Relinquishing our control of our physical, emotional, and relational life makes it possible for us to receive the abundant and eternal life Christ came and comes to offer us.

To lose, *apolesei,* from *apollumi,* is a term borrowed from the world of commerce. Something which was our possession is traded for something else. What we gave up is no longer ours. But in the context of the passage we are considering, what we gain is infinitely more valuable. The exchange of *psuchē* for *zōē* is dramatized in John, chapter 10. Jesus says, "I have come that they may have life, and that they may have it more abundantly" (verse 10).

The life, *psuchē,* He gave on Calvary was to give abundant life, *zōē.* The life of God revealed incarnate in Jesus Christ was imparted to all who would receive because of the atonement of Jesus' physical life as the Lamb of God. The resurrection was God's triumphant validation of that sacrificial death. The love revealed melts our ironclad grip on our psyche. Now, Christ is alive to impart *zōē* to us. Abundant life is the constant flow of His presence around, in, and through us.

The self filled with Christ's *zōē* produces a new person in our physical bodies. That person is alive forever, death has no power over us, and we are free to live with abandoned joy during the days of the brief span of our existence on earth. We know who we are because we know Whose we are. And we can be the person He enables us to be because of His life in us. Fear of being ourselves is gone. Our new self is a manifestation of the reigning Christ. Arrogant or defensive self-confidence is replaced by a winsome and contagious Christ-confidence.

Jim Elliot, the martyred missionary, famously said, "He is

no fool who gives what he cannot keep to gain what he cannot lose." That's our confidence. A life surrendered to Christ becomes His postresurrection home. Our security is not in our adequacy, but in His unlimited power surging through us, changing our personalities, and guiding us in daring expression of the loved, forgiven, transformed person He is enabling us to be. John Henry Newman said, "Fear not that your life will come to an end, but rather that it shall never have a beginning." But the invasion of Christ's *zōē* into our *psuchē* gives us a beginning of true life that nothing can destroy.

One of the most significant results is that we are free from the pressures to be anything other than the new creation Christ is producing in us. Doing His will becomes the joy of our lives. We are not distressed in life's decisions because we can depend on His guidance.

Christ does reveal what we are to be and do in each relationship and situation. We can dare to attempt what others would consider impossible because of His unlimited strength surging in and through us. We don't have to be crippled by what we've been, or constricted by our previously negative idea of what is possible. Being ourselves is letting Christ shine through us!

Enjoy Yourself

It is as you open your life to Christ that you become able to truly enjoy yourself—the new Christ-centered self. *To enjoy yourself, allow Christ to enjoy you.*

I am convinced that people who enjoy themselves are those who know the delicious feeling of being enjoyed. A friend of mine is a fun-loving, unself-conscious person who enjoys being the unique miracle the Lord is producing in him. He spreads that contagious delight to others around him. His ministry of encouragement never seems to bog down in self-condemnation issuing in negativism. He's not the person he used to be, and he's not yet all that the Lord has planned for him to be. But he is a joyful person, free to enjoy himself.

Often, our enjoyment of ourselves is debilitated because we don't like the way we look, or by lack of self-affirmation because of physical limitations. We dislike ourselves because we are too tall or too short, or have some disability that makes us think of ourselves as unattractive. Reading between the lines of Paul's writings, we sense he was not a first-century Charlton Heston. And so he could say, "We have this treasure in earthen vessels, that the excellence of the power may be of God and not of us" (2 Corinthians 4:7). The treasure of Christ's Spirit in the apostle was more important than the vessel.

The other day, I visited a fellow pastor who is one of our nation's most able communicators. He has a receding hairline. I seldom notice this because of the radiance of his face. On the wall next to the mirror in a private restroom attached to his office is an embroidered plaque. On it are these words: *God made a few perfect heads. Others He covered with hair.* There's a man who can enjoy himself coupling a look in the mirror with a laugh at himself.

I am constantly amazed at how few people enjoy themselves. Their freedom to know and be themselves is frustrated by the earthen vessel rather than the power of the Lord which it can contain. The result is that we become more concerned about how we look or come across to others than allowing Christ to shine through the vessel.

The same thing can happen to us because of our remorse over mistakes and failures. "How can the Lord love and use a person who did or said that?" we demand of ourselves in self-incrimination. But He does. None of us is perfect. Good thing. Our pride over our self-generated purity would make us unusable. The Lord delights in surprising the world around us with what He can do with the imperfect people like us.

When we acknowledge that, we can give the Lord the glory. Our enjoyment of being used in spite of our limitations will spill over to other people. The task of the local congregation is not to convince people of how bad they are, but how powerful God is.

A conversation with a friend drifted into concern about a mutual friend. He is a very gifted man who is plagued with lack of self-esteem. My friend said, "I wish that guy enjoyed himself more!" My response was, "Perhaps the place for us to begin to help him is to tell him how much we enjoy him. There's a lot about him I do enjoy." After that conversation I thought long and hard about the people in my life who need to know that I enjoy them. I decided to tell them so—to express my feelings so they would know.

Express Yourself

Finally, when we know who we are, dare to be ourselves, and enjoy the unique miracle each of us is, *we are free to express ourselves.* Under the Lord's guidance we can set our priorities and goals, arrange our lives on His agenda, and do what He has led us to desire for our lives. We don't have to be victims of people or circumstances. Even those situations that seem like limitations to our free self-expression can, by His grace and power, be turned into opportunities to communicate the real person inside us He is enabling us to be. That freedom is spelled out in the dynamics of honesty, directness, and genuineness.

By honesty, I mean the freedom to allow other people to know us. Being honest is the opposite of pretense and posturing. Honesty is vulnerability. The Lord loves us as we are, but has not chosen to leave us as we are. Therefore, we are people in transition. The best of what we are to become is still to be. We are free to admit our shortcomings and problems. No one has it all together. So why should we pretend we have? There is a relaxed, winsome freedom about honest people. They are open about their failures and as a result fail less. The tight

spring of self-generated perfectionism has
been unwound. They are free to make life a
continuous series of new beginnings.

*We don't have to
do an equivocat-
ing "duty dance"
to be liked...
In Christ, we
are more than
liked, we are
loved profoundly.*

That enables directness. We can state
what we believe and want from life because our convictions have been shaped by
time with the Lord in prayer, reflection on
our goals by reading the Bible, and a deep
commitment of our wills to seek and do
the Lord's will. Since our self-esteem is no longer dominated
by people's vacillating opinions or manipulative criticism, we
don't have to do an equivocating "duty dance" to be liked.
People who spend their energies trying to be liked usually
don't like themselves. In Christ, we are more than liked, we
are loved profoundly.

And that quality of acceptance and cherishing esteem frees
us to be genuine. Real, authentic. People will begin to appreciate the consistency. When they discover that integrity in us,
rooted in Christ, they will relate with greater directness with
us. They will not have to squander precious energy worrying
about what we really mean or desire. Most of all, they will
never have to wonder about our love for them. Christ's love
in us will become the consistent, reliable basis of our attitudes
toward them.

Being this kind of free person may seem like an impossibility. Each of us knows how far he is from that quality of freedom. Admitting that is the first step. And that brings us back to the person who is the theme of this book: Christ. *Think freedom, and think clearly about your freedom in Christ, His atonement, righteousness in Him, the power of His indwelling Spirit, and His absolutely reliable strength for all of life.*

Feelings follow thought. Think freedom in Christ, and then feel freely, forgive freely, act freely, receive freely, and dream freely. Remembering always that "the Lord is the Spirit, and where the Spirit of the Lord is, there is freedom" (2 Corinthians 3:17 NIV).

May the Lord
Go Above You

9

Above You to Watch over You

…to Give You the Time of Your Life

The fourth dimension of the essence of the Lord's presence is that He is above us to watch over us. Perhaps this is the most familiar image of His omnipresence. From the time we were children we were taught that He watches over us while we sleep and when we are awake. We cherish the assurance, "May the LORD *watch* between you and me when we are absent one from another" (Genesis 31:49). In the wakeful, restless hours of the night we repeat with Job, "He watches all my paths" (Job 33:11), and with the psalmist, "When I remember You on my bed, I meditate on You in the night watches. Because You have been my help, therefore in the shadow of Your wings I will rejoice. My soul follows close behind You; Your right hand upholds me" (Psalm 63:6-8).

These Old Testament assurances were but a prelude to the time when our risen Savior, the reigning Lord of all, would express His sovereignty in watching over us. His goal is to enable us to have the time of our lives. The double entendre is intended. He wants us to know how precious time is and how He watches over us seeking to help us experience His intervention in our time, and always on time.

"We're having the time of our lives!" These words were written in a note from a couple who had been through rocky times in their marriage. Fortunately, they had discovered God's grace and rediscovered each other through the crisis.

As I read their letter, which burst with joy in every line, I thought about their words, "We're having the time of our lives!" It made me think about the gift of time. I reflected on what I was doing with the time of my life, not just the spectacular moments or special experiences I might describe as "the time of my life," but all of the time given to me. Then it hit me: *Shouldn't I be able to say about every hour, I'm having the time of my life?*

I have to admit that I have lots of hours and many days that are routine or filled with hard work and a busy schedule. It's easy to drift into not expecting the "time of our lives" delight in what we call the mundane. So often we limit those great times to long-awaited vacations, trips, or anticipated auspicious occasions. The result is that we have a lot of uneventful, dull responsibilities between our exciting experiences.

Opportunity and Serendipity

And yet, knowing that Christ is watching over us should enable us to live with expectancy all of the time. He's constantly opening doors of opportunity for us. Our privilege is to make the most of every hour by walking through the open doors to grasp the opportunity the Lord has planned. Who knows—it might be the time of our life—one of millions of them. But sometimes we just don't see those open doors because we are only expecting the commonplace in life.

We say with Pogo, "We are surrounded with insurmountable opportunities."

Too often we echo William Hale White who said, "When I look back over my life and call to mind what I might have had simply for the taking, and did not take, my heart is like to break." In contrast, it was said of Lord Nelson, the hero of Trafalgar, that when opportunity flitted by him, he was always ready and grasped it.

The Latin word for *opportunity* is *opportunitas*. It is a combination of *Op,* meaning before, and *portus,* a port or harbor. The word picture is of an open channel, an incoming tide, and an invitation for a ship to sail into port for a safe anchorage.

So here's a working definition for opportunity—it's a confluence of circumstances that makes a certain action possible with the potential of a timely blessing from Christ.

John Dewey said that the highest mark of intelligence is to recognize and grasp a genuine opportunity. I'd say that it's a sure sign that we've begun to live in the essence of Christ's presence when through His Spirit at work in us we can see and grasp the opportunities provided us every day and every hour. There are opportunities to care for the people around us, carry their burdens, maximize their joy, listen, share our faith, speak out, or take a stand on a justice issue. We never know when a mundane hour will turn out to be a momentous time for us. Christ's blessings aren't predictable; He enjoys surprising us with serendipities!

In 1754 Horace Walpole read a Persian fairy tale that brought springtime joy into his life. In a letter he told about the "thrilling approach to life" the folk tale had given him and how it had helped him recapture an expectant excitement about his daily work.

The tale was about three princes of Ceylon who had set out in search of great treasures. Though they did not find the treasure, they were constantly surprised along the way by more magnificent treasures they had not anticipated.

The ancient name of the island of Ceylon is Serendip, which accounts for the title of the fascinating story of unanticipated discoveries—"The Three Princes of Serendip." From this, Walpole coined the word *serendipity*. It explained a reality that he had known through his studies and work. His most significant and valued experiences had happened to him while he was least expecting them.

The same is true in our experience of the essence of Christ's presence. A serendipity is the breakthrough of Christ into our usual circumstances, the surprise that occurs to us when we are seeking to know Him and be His faithful disciples.

A serendipitous life is distinguished by *surprisability*. A ninth Beatitude might be, "Blessed are those who are surprisable, for the unexpected always happens." When we lose our capacity to be surprised we settle into life's rut of responsibilities and demands with the terrible conviction that we must do everything ourselves. We expect very little and are not disappointed; we aim at nothing and we hit it. One thing I know about Christ, He delights to surprise us with serendipities we never expected.

Paul knew this, and in Ephesians 5:13-20 he gives us four ways to make each day the time of our life.

Buy Up the Time of Your Life

The first is to buy up the time, "Redeeming the time, because the days are evil" (Ephesians 5:16). The Greek word Paul uses for "redeeming," *exagorazo,* is a term from the world of commerce meaning "to purchase or buy up." The word for time is *kairos,* meaning the strategic hour, the seasonable time. It is event-oriented time, the propitious moment for something to happen, *Kairos* is unlike the other Greek word for time, *chronos,* which means linear time measured by length. It is in the passage of *chronos* time that the *kairos* events happen. The word *kairos* is also translated as "opportunity" in other verses. The New International Version, therefore, is also correct in translating Paul's phrase "redeeming the time" as "make the most of every opportunity."

Every day you and I encounter people in trouble—friends with heartaches beneath their polished surfaces, fellow workers who long for someone to care. The Lord has deployed us in our families, workplaces, churches, and communities so we can be used decisively when He wants to communicate His love, forgiveness, and sometimes confrontational truth. I have a friend who begins every day with the prayer, "Lord, make me usable, put me where I can be used, help me be useful so when this day ends, I won't feel useless!"

Buying up the time is something like working on the floor of the stock exchange. Quick decisions must be made under great pressure with many distractions.

We need wisdom and discernment to know what to do or say to make the most of every opportunity. Paul reminds us of our purpose of buying up time—"because the days are evil."

Indeed they are. No one needs to convince us of the influence of Satan over people and situations. And since his schemes are so subtle in holding back the forward movement of the kingdom of God, we need daily, hourly guidance and power. No wonder Paul goes on to say, "Therefore do not be unwise, but understand what the will of the Lord is" (verse 17).

The word for "unwise" really means without reason, a reckless and careless pattern of thinking. In other words, Paul says we should not try to make the most of every opportunity without consistent patterning by the Lord. We are in a battle with Satan, who does not easily release his grip on people and circumstances we want to win for Christ.

The Lord has a strategy for each situation and relationship. Prolonged time in prayer prepares us for them. Often the Lord shows us beforehand what we are to say and do. Other times, He reveals His will at that moment. We don't need to excuse ourselves from a conversation or meeting for private prayer, for when we open the channel of our minds to the Lord daily, we can expect the fulfillment of His promise, "Do not worry about how or what you should answer, or what you should say. For the Holy Spirit will teach you in that very hour what you ought to say" (Luke 12:11). That assurance brings us to Paul's next encouragement for the time of our life.

Spirit-Intoxicated

We are to keep on being filled with the Holy Spirit. "Do

not be drunk with wine, in which is dissipation; but be filled with the Spirit" (Ephesians 5:18). We are to be Spirit-intoxicated Christians.

In Asia Minor, where the cult of Dionysus, the god of wine, was rampant, the Christians were being beguiled with the idea that intoxication with wine was a means to inspiration. Perhaps some of them had been in the cult prior to becoming Christians. Instead of intoxication with wine, Paul calls the Christians to "be filled with the Spirit."

The people to whom Paul wrote had been sealed by the Spirit with an initial infilling and had had repeated fresh infillings each new day and for each new challenge.

Note Paul's use of a certain Greek verb form—the present passive imperative. Being filled with the Spirit is for now, is done *for us* rather than *by us,* and is to be energetically asked for. "Keep on being filled" is the sense of Paul's admonition. This is the real secret of making the most of every hour and of every opportunity.

From Acts we know that the disciples were filled at Pentecost with the Spirit and had repeated fresh infillings. Just as yesterday's stale grace will not do for today's pressures, so, too, our previous experience of the Spirit's inspiration will not suffice for the new challenges that come to us. Nor can we store up the Spirit as if we were reservoirs or holding tanks for spiritual power to be released at our will. Rather, we are to live daily in the flow of Christ's Spirit, power, gifts, and fruit.

A friend explained how he discovered the hourly filling of Christ's Spirit. "I was one of those Christians who took great pride in my baptism by the Spirit. I loved to talk about the assurances and excitement I felt when the Spirit filled me. But I was living in the past. Now I've realized that was for then, to get me moving. Now to stay moving, I need a new anointing every day…and over and over again throughout the day."

Christ's indwelling Spirit makes us wide awake to opportunities and gives us the freedom to enter into the present moment knowing we'll have exactly what we need.

And remember that the indwelling Spirit is Himself the joy we need. So having the time of our life throughout each day is something that happens in us regardless of the grimness of people or circumstances around us.

Sing Your Way Through the Day

The indefatigable joy of Christ enables us to sing our way through the day. Paul suggests that we speak "to one another in psalms and hymns and spiritual songs, singing and making melody in your heart to the Lord" (Ephesians 5:19).

It's what we sing that makes the difference. Paul recommends spiritual songs, hymns, and psalms. There's a wealth of all three to express the song in our hearts. How about, "This is the day the Lord has made, I will rejoice and be glad in it," or "Bless the Lord, oh my soul and bless His holy name, forget not all His blessings," or "He is Lord, He is Lord, He is risen from the dead and He is Lord," or "In my life, Lord, be glorified"? The resources seem limitless.

I find it helpful to add to my morning devotions a psalm and a hymn or a contemporary spiritual song. One of them is sure to speak to my need and become my theme song for the day. Sometimes we have a repetitive thought that captures our mind for several days. And sometimes it's negative and depressing. Why not replace it with a song of joy that puts hope in our hearts and rhythm in our steps. It will help us claim the next amazing way that Paul suggests for having the time of our lives—all day long.

Thanksgiving Day Every Hour

Thanksgiving really puts things into perspective. Paul encourages "giving thanks always for all things to God the Father in the name of our Lord Jesus Christ" (Ephesians 5:20).

Thanks always? Yes. Nothing maximizes our delights and minimizes our discouragements like thanksgiving. It is an antidote to any pride we might feel or a medicine for painful problems. When we thank the Lord, we enjoy what He has done for us in obvious blessings and anticipate what He will do when life gets bumpy. Thanksgiving for our difficulties is really a method of commitment, a trust that the Lord will use everything to draw us into deeper oneness with Him. Thanksgiving brings release from the tension of having to take credit for our accomplishments and produces resolve to move on to discover the growth we'll experience in our adversities. This is no silly palliative, but the source of power!

You and I have been called to redeem the time, to make the most of every opportunity. It's not just Paul's idea, or mine; it's the Lord's plan for claiming the essence of His presence. So why not have the time of your life—all the time?

10

Above You to Ensure You Live Now and Forever

*The experience of the essence of Christ's presence
is to live life to the fullest now…and forever.*

Jesus Christ came to live, reveal, and offer us both the abundant life and eternal life. You and I want both! But the second is dependent on the first. In fact, both express the same reality: life in Christ lived to the fullest, both now and beyond the comma in life we call death.

In our search to know and do the will of God, so much is answered by this simple formula: The will of God is that we live to the fullest both in this life and forever in heaven. We have a vague idea of what that means. But we get hassled with the pressures and stresses of life and end so many days feeling that we have existed but have not lived.

So many Christians confess to me that though they feel

fairly sure of eternal life, they don't experience what they suspect Jesus meant by the abundant life. Even after conversion, they continue to be wracked with worry, pressured by conflicting demands, and unsatisfied by what their relationships provide or they are able to give to them. As one church member said to me recently, "I'm not as worried about dying in the end as I am about being half-dead right now!"

Christ wants to set us free to experience the liberating truth that whatever enables joyous, adventuresome, and courageous living—now and forever—is the will of God. So often we wring our hands in worried search for guidance. Does a choice enable us to grow in Christ and live the abundant life as He lived and taught it? If so, we can press on with the assurance of God's will. If not, it is wasted time ruminating over the possibility. When a choice will stifle Christ's free reign in us or debilitate anyone else's growing relationship with Him, we can be sure it is not the will of God.

Surely there are difficult and painful things we must go through which enable us to grow up as persons. But they are usually clearly defined by obedience to some aspect of discipleship or service which requires faithfulness and follow-through to what Christ has said about losing our lives to find them.

It's time to enter into the full delight of fellowship with Christ, and it's also time to listen carefully to what He said about giving ourselves away lavishly to the needs of others. He has promised to make His home in us. Our response should be to give Him full command and get cracking!

⊶ ⩤⧫⩥ ⊷

In order to do that, we need three things: an assurance that we belong to Christ; a certainty that He lives in us; and an unreserved commitment to live life to the fullest because we know that we are alive forever.

Jesus promised all three in one of His clearest statements of the will of God. The occasion which prompted His forth-right revelation was a conversation with the people who had witnessed the miracle of the feeding of the five thousand. Jesus discerned that they wanted further signs and proofs. What more than the multiplication of the loaves and fishes did they need?

Like so many of us who are in a frenzied search for guidance, they wanted further specifics of what they were to do if they were to do the works of God. But Jesus was very direct: "This is the work of God, that you believe in Him whom He sent." That in itself would be an invigorating inventory for us in our search for the will of God. We could occupy a thousand years of life just spelling out the specifics about which there is no need to wonder.

But Jesus went on. He made a bold messianic claim and

offered bread that satisfies: "For the bread of God is He who comes down from heaven and gives life to the world." Note the emphasis on life! The people responded, "Lord, give us this bread always."

Don't Miss the Reason You Were Born

You and I want to live and not miss the reason we were born. That life is Christ Himself. "I am the bread of life, He who comes to Me shall never hunger, and he who believes in Me shall never thirst." Linger for a moment with me on that momentous statement. Christ is all that we need in every moment of this life so that we can know life at its highest, and then enter into an even greater fullness beyond the grave. This creates the environment in which we can appropriate the specific revelation of the essential will of God which Jesus went on to explain.

Christ's ministry within us is to be sure our wills are liberated and that we have clarity each step of the way regarding what we are to be and do.

Don't miss the uncluttered clarity of this promise: "All that the Father gives Me will come to Me, and the one who comes to Me I will by no means cast out." That is our blessed assurance: We have been elected to belong to Christ. Chosen. Called. He will accomplish His work in us. He will never cast us out. He wants us to live even more than we do! Christ's ministry with us is to be sure our wills are liberated and that we have clarity each step of the way regarding what we are to be and do. We are in good hands!

Start Really Living

Now here is what He came (and comes) to do so we can really start living: "I have come down from heaven, not to do My own will, but the will of Him who sent Me." He continues to say those same words in you and me. His indwelling presence molds our wills around His own and guides us in every decision:

> This is the will of the Father who sent Me, that of all He has given Me I should lose nothing, but should raise it up at the last day. And this is the will of Him who sent Me, that everyone who sees the Son and believes in Him may have everlasting life.

If all we had to go on was that magnificent promise, we would have more than enough. It tells us that God's basic will is our eternal life and that His presence is with us in Christ to get us through the days of this life safely home to heaven. To accomplish that, He went to the cross, rose from the dead, lives in us in the power of His Spirit to abide with us and in us forever.

We experience a grace which captures our thoughts and floods our emotions with uncontainable love—for Him, ourselves, and others. The will is now the ready servant of an entirely new purpose. We want to do the will of the One who loved us and gave His life for us.

In that context, you and I can claim the promises Christ has made about prayer as the channel through which our wills become attuned to His. "If you abide in Me, and My words abide in you, you will ask what you desire, and it shall be done for you" (John 15:7). We so often leap to the second part of that promise before we meet the qualifying offer of the first part. Jesus and His words must abide in us before we can know what or how to ask. The two-part blessing contains His words, His message available to us to study in the Gospels, and His abiding presence which selects the particular truths we need in any situation and helps us clarify for what we should ask. Abiding in Christ and allowing Him to abide in us is the secret for guidance. It means to make Him our dwelling and to open our minds as His dwelling—to rest, relax, and receive. This habitual abiding, punctuated by consistent times of prayer and study of His Word, will get us ready for the decisions and choices we have to make.

My Own Experience

Allow me to share an insight that came to me years ago and has been updated by experiences ever since. One day I was unsure of the will of God in my life. When I prayed, all that came to me were the words, *The restless search for the will of God is a sure sign you are out of it!* You can imagine that this was not a very comforting answer to my prayer for an unde-niable word from the Lord for the decisions I had to make! I mulled the words over for weeks. They led me to a confession that my walk with the Lord had become dull and perfunctory. Several areas of my life were not in good order. I had moved from trusting to strenuous effort to do God's work. My life was more self-effort than a flow of the Lord's grace.

Then when I needed clarity of God's will for my life, I went to Him seeking an answer. But none came—only the insight articulated in the words just shared with you. Because of the interruption in my communion with the Lord and my resistance to what I already knew was His will for me in other areas, I was not able to convince the Lord to give me what I wanted. He had not closed me out; I had closed Him out.

During the weeks that followed, I got reacquainted with Christ. I allowed Him to take charge of the corridors of my mind I had closed off. The less I focused on getting the answer to my particular question for immediate guidance, the greater clarity came as to what I should do. The Lord's will for me was to abide, listen, and wait—to want *Him* more than His guidance. Out of love for me, He withheld temporarily what I *wanted* in order to give me what I *needed.*

Can you identify with that personal account? Perhaps it speaks to what you're facing right now. The words the Lord gave me—"The restless search for the will of God is a sure sign you're out of it"—may sound harsh and insensitive. But let them seep into the tissues of the cortex of your brain. Allow them to focus your thought and then congeal into your will. The One who revealed the essential will of God that we live the abundant life and the eternal life wants to abide in you and me more deeply than ever before.

It is reassuring to know that the Lord is the same yesterday, today, and tomorrow. It is equally liberating to know that He sees the decisions and choices we are going to have to make. Is it not reasonable to assume that He wants to get us ready?

Tough Decisions

Think of a time when you came up to a really tough decision and knew immediately what you were supposed to do. Remember the delight you felt in being able to be decisive? Chances are very good that the Lord had been getting you ready. Time with Him had clarified your values. His abiding presence had given a healthy sense of self-esteem. You felt good about yourself and your future. There were no complicating areas of resistance to the Lord which drained off your energy and attention, seeking to interpose themselves as the issue of your present choice. Your mind was free of guilt over unconfessed sins. Abiding with Christ had brought those areas of disagreement to the surface, and they had been resolved with confession and forgiveness. You felt free, assured, in tune with the Lord, and the act of will crystalliz-ing your thought seemed obvious. What in other times would have been a source of turmoil in seeking the Lord's will was obviously the way to go, and you exercised your will with freedom and assurance.

Is it too much to expect that this is the way Christ wants us to live consistently?

Unless I miss my guess, you are probably thinking, *Yes, but some things are more difficult than others. There are times when I'm really up against it and don't know the Lord's will for my life.*

But is anything too big for Him? Does He will the an-guished times of uncertainty? He has all power in heaven and earth! The long period we endure wrestling is often caused by the difficulty of bringing our wills into alignment with His, rather than by His reluctance to show us the way.

A woman said to me, "I don't know what Christ is waiting for! It has taken Him so long to make His will plain in this situation. I'm ready; I only wish He were!"

Was He not ready? Did He not know the resolution of the problem in that situation? Or was He waiting for this woman to be made ready?

In fact, that was exactly the case. The timing was not right; she was running ahead of the Lord. When He had her cool her heels and got her in harmony with His abiding presence, she saw the answer which had been waiting there all along!

Our Three Basic Desires

The will of the Lord that we should live—now and for-ever—is perfectly congruent with the three basic desires that He has placed in us. We all want to be maximum in the real-ization of our potential; we all quest to enjoy the years of our life to the fullest; and we all long for the assurance that this life is but a brief part of eternity for us. The zest for life is the endowment of the Lord of all life.

The apostle John was moved to stunning rhetoric about that wondrous blend of our need and Christ's provision:

> In Him was life, and the life was the light of men...As many as received Him, to them He gave the right to become chil-dren of God, to those who believe in His name: who were born, not of blood, nor of the will of the flesh, nor of the will of man, but of God (John 1:4,12-13).

Life as Christ lived it and life as He lives it in us is the only way to satisfy our real desires and His demands. He is God's will for us. That will is perfect in that it affirms our potential, accomplishes our purpose, and assures us of perpetuity.

Perfect by Christ's Presence

Our longing for perfection can be met only as the One who is perfect takes up residence in us. The word *perfect* in the Greek means "end" or "goal." Christ dwelling in us is the Maxi-mizer of all our potential. As the Wisdom of God, He inspires our thinking. As the Power of God, He infuses us with the willing, engendering strength to seek and want to follow His guidance. His ministry in our lives is to help us face the opportunities and challenges of life on His power. And nothing is impossible for Him!

Next consider your desire to know and accomplish your purpose. Again Christ is our Guide. He focuses for us our ultimate purpose to be His person and to glorify Him in all that we do. His message charts the way, showing us how to love others and give ourselves away in service. The needs of people and their suffering become our deep concern. Their longing to live abundantly becomes the motive of sharing what Christ has meant to us. And moment-by-moment, daily guidance is given by His abiding, indwelling presence.

Paul expressed the basic purpose for which we were born: "Let this mind be in you which was also in Christ Jesus" (Philippians 2:5). With that gift, our purpose and all our plans to reach it will be sorted out and sifted and made one with the Lord's will.

And finally, our fear of death and the desperate need of an assurance of perpetuity are more than satisfied in the risen Christ. He defeated the powers of death and rose from the grave. Because He lives, we live also—forever. Death for you and me is behind us. It occurred when we surrendered our lives—mind, emotion, will, and body—to the Lord. Our funeral, celebrating the death of willfulness, was also the joyous day of our rebirth. By the will of the Lord and not our own strength, "You He *made alive,* who were dead in trespasses and sins" (Ephesians 2:1). And now we are free to live life—the resurrected life—by the power of the Lord with us.

Thus we can see how perfectly Christ fulfilled His task and continues to fulfill it in us today. Nothing God wants or we need has been left out. Our only challenge is to accept it and begin living in it. And He even provides that! He is above us to help us live now and forever!

May the Lord
Go Within You

11

The Character
Transplant

...the Miracle of the New You

May the living Christ go *in* you. This final phrase in the benediction I delight in giving is the assurance of the most stupendous promise Christ ever made. He promised to make His
postresurrection home in us. Christianity is not only life in
Christ as recipients of the efficacy of His atoning death and
victorious resurrection, but it also is the life of Christ in us.

This astounding truth is based on Christ's own words. He
promised to abide in us. "Abide in Me and I in you...without
Me you can do nothing" (John 15:4-5). Our commitment to
Christ is only a beginning. He longs to give us more and more.
Remember He said, "To him who has will more be given,
and he will have abundance" (Matthew 13:12 RSV). Once we

have the assurance of eternal life, we are ready to receive the blessing of abundant life. If life is Christ, then abundant life must be more of Him. To be in Christ as a believer, disciple, and loved and forgiven person is one thing. To have Christ in us as motivator, enabler and transformer of our character is something more. Much more!

William Law, who taught John Wesley at Oxford, put it succinctly, "A Christ not in us is a Christ not ours." Not what, but Whom. Not someday, but now. Not near, but here. Not only Christ with us, but Christ in us.

A Christ-captivated life enables us to live an extraordinary life. We are not limited to the confines of our own intellect or talent. The secret is Christ in us. Paul discovered that and communicated the wonder of the transferred life when he wrote to the Colossians about the mystery hidden for ages but now manifested in Christ's people: "Christ in you, the hope of glory" (Colossians 1:27). Glory is manifestation. Christ manifests Himself in us and transforms us into His own image. The secret of the Christian life is not only that we have been *with* Jesus but that He is in us! There should be daily amazement—first in us and then in others—as to what we are able to discern, dare, and do. Christ in us is the inner source of wisdom beyond human sagacity, discernment beyond our human analysis, love beyond our cautious affection, truth beyond our previous, limited experience. The deeper we grow in Christ, the more people will be forced to wonder.

There is a figure of speech in the New Testament that has an agrarian, almost archaic sound. It seems strangely out of sync in vocabularies of Christians living in the twenty-first century—in a technological society where one branch of science is preparing us for life in the galaxies, and another claims to be moving closer to producing a disease-free race of "ideal" human beings by means of the precise manipulation of human genes.

The figure of speech I refer to is "fruit of the Spirit." Far from being obsolete, the idea captured in this image resembles and yet transcends the temporal promises of the technologies I have just mentioned as a candle flame is transcended by the sun!

"Fruit of the Spirit" is the special term the apostle Paul uses for the spiritual "transplant" that takes place when the character of Christ is formed and begins to grow in men and women destined to live beyond time and space in resurrected bodies. The power dimension is in the fruit of the Spirit, coming as a result of Christ in us and making us like Himself.

It is absolutely impossible to live within our own strength the kind of life Christ has called us to live. No amount of

Falseness...results when the word Christian *becomes an adjective for a self-conscious lifestyle instead of a person fully alive because of empowerment by the Spirit of Christ.*

culture, education, or effort on our part that is not empowered by the Spirit of Christ can produce Christian character.

There is nothing more tragic than a vision without the power to live it and nothing more debilitating than the discovery that the demands of becoming a vital Christian are too much for this genetic combination we call "self." We end up being inauthentic people, prisoners of the falseness that results when the word *Christian* becomes an adjective for a self-conscious lifestyle instead of a person fully alive because of empowerment by the Spirit of Christ.

In a world without antibiotics, computers, cellular phones, and PDAs, God's Son fleshed out the authentic graces of love, joy, peace, patience, kindness, goodness, faithfulness, gentleness, and self-control. And it was in observing the quality of these earthly, everyday character traits in Christians of his world that Paul made this profound theological affirmation about the miracle of the character transplant.

How did Paul choose this amazing symbol of the fruit of the Spirit? Did it come in a flash of inspiration, or did he reflect long and hard before he selected the word *fruit* from ordinary language as a symbol for this hidden life force? In any case, the choice is not out of character with the way he thought and taught. He coined the phrase "eyes of the heart" as a takeoff from eyes of the body, why not a progression from fruit of the body to "fruit of the Spirit"?

Paul's special phrase concerns itself primarily with the *process* of growth. Whether in the soil, in the soft, silent womb, or deep in the human spirit, all new births have something in common. Each is intricately programmed for growth, but all require the cooperation of forces and environments outside themselves to reach their potential. And so does the miraculous growth process of the fruit of the Spirit.

The implications behind Paul's special term are radical. They are also profoundly personal. Would you like to experience the deep energy of pure love and joy? Could the parched quality of your life be replenished with the soft dew of peace? Do you need to be patient in some relationship? There is auxiliary power for all of that and more. There is new power to arrest the countdown for those debilitating emotional blast-offs, new courage to risk gentleness without fear of being exploited, and reinforcement for diminishing self-control.

<hr />

In the previous four sections of this book, we've talked about the Lord going before, behind, beside, and above us. Now we are ready to experience the essence of His presence within us. I often think of the ninefold fruit of the Spirit as

Christ seeking really to bless us. Here, indeed, is the essence of Christ's presence.

May the Lord go within you to give you love, joy, peace, patience, kindness, goodness, faithfulness, gentleness, self-control.

The rest of this book is about the continuing life of Jesus Christ in you and me. I invite you to do more than read it. Experience it. Let the world see once again the radiance of the essence of His presence in you!

12

Within You to Give You Extraordinary Love

May Christ go in you to love through you.

Jesus Christ came to reveal extraordinary living. He called a new breed of humanity to live in Him and allow Him to live in them. The extraordinary life consists in receiving and communicating extraordinary love: Christ's love as He lived it; His love in us; and our love for others motivated by Him.

It is important to note that Paul does not pluralize the word *fruit* in his special term. He does not say: "The *fruits* of the Spirit *are*..." To do so would seem to destroy the unity of the image he has chosen to illustrate the power of Christ's life force within us. The word *fruit* is singular for a second reason. It represents the one and only source from which Christlike character can flow—the Spirit of Christ Himself.

The fruit of the Spirit is love.

Paul selected a Greek word for "love" that is generally used to express divine love as distinct from human love or friendship. This divine dimension of extraordinary love will affect all loves, but we are called to be containers and transmitters of Christ's love to the world. The life and message of Christ reveals it; His presence in us elevates us beyond the ordinary to experience and express it. This love, which is a fruit of His dwelling within us, is unmerited, lived on the millionth mile, and impossible for us on our own.

The extraordinary love Jesus requires in the Sermon on the Mount is what He inspires in us when He comes to make His home in us. Jesus expressed this love throughout His life, and His Spirit makes such love possible in the extraordinary lovers who have come to be known as Christians.

Impossible Love?

The disciples were astonished when they first heard about this divine dimension of love. It is not the kind of love that comes naturally for people. It is the kind of love that gives us resiliency in our resentment and releases others from recrimination. The love Jesus taught is more than family affection *(storgē);* far more than the passion of physical love *(erōs);* infinitely more than warm friendship *(philia).* Christ's love is unconquerable acceptance and benevolence for people, regardless of what they do or who they are.

The Sermon on the Mount confronts us with the essential

nature of this love. It is unmotivated. Nothing that the recipient does, or refuses to do, stirs its sublime power. Just as God's love for us in Christ was not motivated by our accomplishments or adequacy, so, too, the fruit of Christ's love in us is a love that is not motivated by the person who needs it. That's what makes it extraordinary! It comes from Christ. His Spirit in us is the only motivation. Matthew 5:38-48 is our charter, offering the secret of love for people we resent and those who have become our enemies. Read it again in preparation for our consideration of the gift of unmotivated love we want to claim in this chapter.

I once talked to a man who was being eaten alive by his resentments. In an hour's conversation, he said 20 times, directly or indirectly, that he was resentful. I counted! He had come to see me about a growing sense of anxiety. The cause became obvious: He had turned his resentments inward on himself. Because he said he was a Christian, he had forbidden himself ever to get angry. But he was angry—at people, at life in general and, in a way, at God. The virus of resentment had attacked his soul. And resentment, like revenge, is not sweet. It is poisonous!

How about you? Do you ever feel put upon, misused, harmed, misunderstood, taken for granted? How do you handle it when people do or say things which hurt or hinder you? Listen to your own words. "I resent that!" "I resent what he does!" "I resent the way you relate to me!"

In this passage from the Sermon on the Mount, Jesus reiterates the *lex talionis* or ordinary love. "You have heard that it was said, 'An eye for an eye and a tooth for a tooth'" (Matthew 5:38). This law was based on Exodus 21:23-24: "You shall give life for life, eye for eye, tooth for tooth, hand for hand, foot for foot, burn for burn, wound for wound, stripe for stripe." This may seem harsh, but it actually represented a step toward mercy. In the ancient world, it was common for an injured person to wipe out the whole tribe of the person who had harmed or maligned him. This law of Moses went beyond that to an exact *quid pro quo.* Later, even that became refined by the development of the *Baba Kamma,* in which the courts decided the payment of money for injury.

Love as a Response to Insult

But here is Jesus with an alarming, astounding challenge. He calls for no retaliation at all! "I tell you not to resist an evil person" (verse 39). That means, "Don't get involved in active retaliation against people who do evil toward you." He then makes it very specific in four kinds of insults that cause us to be resentful.

Insults to Our Dignity

"Whoever slaps you on your right cheek, turn the other to him also." A right-handed person standing in front of another person would have to use the back of his or her hand to strike the blow. According to rabbinic law, to hit a person with the back of the hand was twice as insulting as to hit him or her with the flat of the hand.

The insults we suffer come not so much from the flat of the hand as from the words flatly spoken to or about us. And Jesus says offer the other cheek. Now we see why we need the un-motivated quality of extraordinary love. What insults linger in your memory? When things people have said drift back to us through the gossip network, we feel anger and resentment. We want to get back at the person, return the volley. We hurt.

We need the fruit of love when forgiveness is required. Only a fresh experience of Christ's forgiveness can enable us to forgive and not return a retributive insult. Or we say, "I'll forgive, but I won't forget!" That is just another way of saying that we will not forgive. Only Christ can help us fulfill Paul's challenge, "Be kind to one another, tenderhearted, forgiving one another, even as God in Christ forgave you" (Ephesians 4:32). Forgiveness was so crucial to the Master that it was the only dimension of the Lord's Prayer He reiterated for emphasis:

> If you forgive men their trespasses, your heavenly Father will also forgive you. But if you do not forgive men their trespasses, neither will your Father forgive your trespasses (Matthew 6:14-15).

The parable of the unmerciful servant nails that down

tighter than we would like. A king wanted to settle his accounts with debtors. One owed him 10,000 talents. A talent was worth about $1000—so $10 million total! What a debt! We are shocked. The debtor could not possibly pay. The king followed the law of the land: The servant and his family were sentenced to slavery. And yet, when the man begged the king for mercy, the debt was forgiven. We would expect that servant to be the most magnanimous man alive after that.

Instead, immediately he went to find one of his debtors who owed him 100 denarii—20 dollars at most. He demanded payment. What a contrast—$20 versus $10 million! When the servant's debtor could not pay, he took him by the throat, throttled him, and threw him into prison.

The point of Jesus' story is not what the king's servant did before his forgiveness, it was what he did afterward. But news like that travels fast. It got back to the king who revoked his previous forgiveness and handed the servant over, not just to prison, but to the torturers.

The conclusion of the parable is frightening. We cannot tear it from our Bibles. Jesus said, "So My heavenly Father also will do to you if each of you, from his heart, does not forgive his brother his trespasses" (Matthew 18:35). That shakes us in our boots! The word *heart* is the key. Only the fruit of love, Christ's love, can give us the power to forgive from our hearts. When our hearts are His home, He does the forgiving through us. Alexander Pope was right: "To err is human, to forgive divine."

Freed from Defensiveness

Next, Jesus focuses on the invasion of a person's rights. "If any one wants to sue you and take away your tunic, let him have your cloak also" (Matthew 5:40). The coat, or tunic as other translations render it, was a *chitōn,* a long inner garment of cotton or linen. Most people had several of these. The cloak was more valuable: it was a great, blanketlike garment worn as outer clothing by day and used as a blanket by night. Ancient Hebrew law protected this possession:

> If you ever take your neighbor's garment as a pledge, you shall return it to him before the sun goes down. For that is his only covering, it is his garment for his skin. What will he sleep in? (Exodus 22:26-27).

To sue a man for his tunic was to take him to court for all he had. It is like saying, "I'll sue you right down to the clothes on your back!" or "I'll take you for everything you've got!" When someone does that, Jesus says, offer him your cloak also. Give him your pledge. Tell him that you want to get to the bottom of his grievances and settle the matter. He is calling for freedom from defensiveness. When our security is in Him, we can look at accusations honestly. We are liberated to admit where we have failed and be graciously open where we have not. What a wonderful way to live!

The fruit of love is communicated in a desire to see things as they are. Fortified by the power of such love, we can say to people who accuse us, "Listen, you feel you have a right to this because of what you think I've done to you. I want to hear you out, and I promise to seek your forgiveness if, after the whole matter is exposed, I have acted wrongly." Or we can say, "You have a grievance against me, I give you my pledge that I want to know what you perceive I've done and settle the matter." In other words, "If I've hurt you, I want to know how. You have a right to your feelings. I want to know what I might have done." No ordinary love, that!

I have great admiration for the founders of the Christian Legal Society, an organization which seeks to help Christians in the negotiation of conflicts which otherwise could end up in long and costly court battles. My esteemed friend Robert Toms, one of the nation's top attorneys, is one of the founders. Along with others, he has fleshed out Jesus' admonition, "Agree with your adversary quickly, while you are on your way with him, lest your adversary deliver you to the judge" (Matthew 5:25). These Christian lawyers help people demonstrate the essence of the presence of Christ's extraordinary love in conflicts. People are encouraged to admit that there are two sides to every issue, and are helped to enter into prayerful negotiation, transforming lose-lose situations into win-win resolutions. The most formidable challenge is always to set people free of defensiveness.

Christ in us can free us of truncated vision. He gives us double vision to look at ourselves and the other person. Resentment over the invasion of our rights is cured by a growing sense of righteousness with the Lord.

Our Too-Easily Injured Pride

But what about our pride? Jesus goes on to confront injuries to our pride. He does that with an example familiar to all His listeners in saying that if anyone forces you to go one mile, you should go with him two miles (Matthew 5:41). In Jesus' time, a Roman soldier could lay his sword on the shoulder of any Jew and make him carry a load like a beast of burden. It was an excruciating insult. Roman roads were marked off in one-mile sections. It was as if Jesus was saying, "If a Roman compels you to go a mile, keep the load on your back and astound him by going a second mile." The Greek word *aggareuein* ("compel"), from the word *aggareus*, actually came from the Persian postal service word meaning "courier." The Persian couriers could press people or their property into their service at will. Eventually, the word came to mean the power of an occupying army to conscript a conquered people into the most menial tasks.

When we combine this statement of Jesus with His admonitions about forgiveness to Peter, we realize that He meant not only the second mile, but the millionth mile of living. The reluctant disciple wanted to set limits on forgiveness: "Up to seven times?" The Master's immediate reply was a Hebraism that meant "without limits": "I do not say to you, up to seven times, but up to seventy times seven" (Matthew 18:22). The same is true when our pride is injured by what people do to us.

We feel resentment when people ask us to do something that we think is beneath us because we are overqualified, or when they neglect to ask us to do something for which we are eminently qualified. Our feelings are out-of-sorts too much of the time. The slights and oversights rankle us. We stew in our own emotional juices, all because our security is misplaced. There is no limit to the good we can do when we do not care who gets the glory and recognition. But that takes more than ordinary love.

Intrusions on Our Privacy

The fourth thing Jesus confronts is our reactions to intrusions on our privacy. The three most important human commodities we have are time, experience, and money. We all feel resentment when people demand our time when it is not convenient or when we are under pressure. They impose on us as if they are the only people alive and all we have to do is to be with them. Also, we resent people who refuse to do their own homework and leech on our learning and experience, hammered out in years of hard work. We all feel mixed reactions when we are assailed by poachers, beggars, and friends who want money we have worked hard to earn. Once I was accosted by a man on the street who asked me for a dollar—not for a cup of coffee, but for a beer! Another person on the street said what we all feel at times: "I don't know why these people don't work for a living like the rest of us." But most disturbing are the people who never become independent and are constantly on our doorstep wanting us to support their irresponsibility.

The Ministry of Compassion

Then we hear Jesus' call for extraordinary giving as an expression of love. "Give to him who asks you, and from him who wants to borrow from you do not turn away" (Matthew 5:42). The more I ponder that, the more dependent I am on the Lord to live it. He reminds me that all that I have and am is His gift. Without Him I could not breathe a breath, think a thought, write a sentence, preach a message, earn a dime, or develop my life. All that I have is from Him to be given away lavishly.

We often hear the old shibboleth "You can't take it with you." Wrong! We will take our souls with us into eternity. What we have done with outer resources will dramatically affect the inner person that death cannot destroy. The parable of the rich man and Lazarus drives that frightening point closer to home than we like.

Most people do not need the material things we can give or lend, but rather they need our love. That is the deeper implication of Jesus' admonition. It is easy to give a handout and hope we will never see the person again. Instead of a dollar for a beer for the man on the street, it took ten dollars for a meal and hours of my time, and the members of Alcoholics Anonymous, to set the man free of his compulsive alcoholism by helping him experience Christ's love and forgiveness.

We are channels, not holding tanks, of love. If we get to a place where the resources have run out, we need to check our connection to the Vine.

People who are habitually in need of money really need help to get on their feet. They require prolonged times of counseling and an introduction to the Savior. That means not just our time, but ourselves.

To be free to give ourselves away is the fruit of Christ the Vine. When we are branches attached to the unlimited source of love, we are never alone or without an adequate flow of healing grace for others.

There is a difference between "getting even" and "even getting." One is the way of resentment, the other the way of release. *Getting even* is normal life stretched to the breaking point and severed. *Even getting* is proportionate inflow and outgo—we are never asked to give more than we have received. We are channels, not holding tanks, of love. If we get to a place where the resources have run out, we need to check our connection to the Vine. No root, no fruit!

The Four Steps of Loving

Jesus goes on in the Sermon on the Mount to give us the specific steps of communicating extraordinary love. He does it in contrast to teaching current at the time: "You shall love your neighbor and hate your enemy." His startling challenge was,

> *Love* your enemies, *bless* those who curse you, *do good* to those who hate you, and *pray* for those who spitefully use you and persecute you (Matthew 5:44).

The key to expressing that kind of love is in the experience of the family characteristic of God's character shared with His children: "That you may be sons of your Father who is in heaven" (Matthew 5:45 rsv). Jesus tells us that we can be like God in the communication of His love. I would like to suggest a reordering of the active verbs *love, bless, do good,* and *pray* in a progression that works for me:

1. pray
2. love
3. bless
4. do good

It is consistent with the Lord's total message and gives us some specific steps to take in being extraordinary lovers.

Start with prayer. Talk to the Lord about the person you find it difficult to love; ask the Lord to show you the deeper reason. In conversation, allow Him to give you His perspective on the person and his or her hidden needs you may not have perceived. In the quiet, picture the person as loved by Christ and filled with His Spirit. Claim that it will be so!

Next, ask for the gift of love for that person. Tell the Lord that you cannot love him or her by yourself. Ask for a special infilling of giving and forgiving love that only He can provide.

Now, put that into words to the person. To bless is to belong and to be beloved. We are beloved by Christ and so can bless others. Most people need to hear in words what the Lord has helped us to experience. Answer this question: What could I say that would help that person to know I am for him or her, that nothing can change my attitude? People so desperately need affirmation and encouragement.

Lastly, as a companion to words of love, "do good" to the person. What is the loving act that will make our words believable? The Lord will help us discern what that is. Love is what we do along with what we say.

Whenever we follow these simple, decisive steps, the fruit of love changes us and then our relationships. And we discover that the purpose of our lives is to be loved and to love. *Living is for loving.*

No one can read or digest Jesus' explanation of extraordinary love without exclaiming, "That's impossible!" The response is exactly what Jesus expects and wants. If we could do it by ourselves, we would not need the precious fruit of His love. That leaves us with this perturbing question: What are we attempting in loving others that we could never pull off without the indwelling power of the Lord's love? *We were never meant to be ordinary.* Offering others unmerited love is the authentic hallmark of a Christ-filled Christian.

13

Within You to Give You Lasting Joy

Just imagine it! Jesus' joy in you. Lasting joy.
It's an exhilarating elixir, an antidote to drabness—
an aspect of the essence of His presence.

True joy has nothing to do with gush or ho-ho jolliness. It is more than happiness. It is impervious to difficult situations. Joy is an outward expression of grace, Christ's unmerited love. The Greek word for "grace" is *charis* and the word for "joy" is *chara*. They both come from the same root.

Joy is the second character trait awaiting transplant and development in us, listed under Paul's special term *fruit.*

I want to tackle a disturbing question. Why are there so many dogged, joyless, do-it-yourself Christians? We see them everywhere. Some experience sporadic, fleeting moments of joy, but they are not lasting or consistent. Allow me to suggest a possible answer that has been growing to conviction-sized proportions in my mind.

Joy is the result of being loved by Christ. When His undeserved grace and forgiveness penetrate through the thick layers of self-doubt and self-negation, we begin to feel the surge of joy. Christ-esteem and joy go together. We joyously can exclaim, "I'm glad I'm me!" That's not easy for most Christians. We find it difficult to let Christ love us and change our demeaning self-image. It takes a constant reminder of how much He loves us. The cross alone can balance the scales weighted with self-condemnation.

＊・＋　▆◆▆　＋・＊

But why is it that Christians who know about the grace of Christ repeatedly still miss the joy? There are several reasons: each presses us deeper into an understanding of true joy.

First, there can be no joy without Christ living in us. His promises about joy are all connected to realizing a profound intimacy with Him. Like love, joy flows from the Vine into the branch. When we abide in Him and He in us, we know joy. In John 15, Jesus took great care to explain His "I Am" assertion: that He was the true vine from whom our spiritual vitality flows. Right after that He said, "These things I have spoken to you, that My joy may remain in you, and that your joy may be full" (John 15:11). R. Leonard Small's now-classic words summarize the promise: "Joy is the standard that flies on the battlements of the heart when the King is in residence." Jesus Christ Himself is our joy!

Second, many people miss the joy because they don't expect to experience it in the midst of difficulties. In John 16, Christ told us that we would know sorrow and disappointment, but that it would be a prelude to experiencing a new joy:

> You now have sorrow; but I will see you again and your hearts will rejoice and your joy no one will take from you... Most assuredly, I say to you, whatever you ask the Father in My name He will give you. Until now you have asked nothing in My name. Ask, and you will receive, that your joy may be full (John 16:22-24).

Secret Source of Joy

The conclusion of Jesus' message there in the upper room gives the secret source of His joy. His honest statement about reality is coupled with the assurance of His victory over evil and death. He faced the cross with this assurance: "I am not alone, because the Father is with me" (verse 32). Then He gave the disciples the liberating legacy for joy. "These things I have spoken to you, that in Me you may have peace. In the world you will have tribulation; but be of good cheer, I have overcome the world" (verse 33).

Joy is not something we know only when everything is

smooth and easy. It is not spiritual ecstasy when all our problems are solved. Rather, joy is the special fruit of the indwelling Christ in the actual experience of problems. The reason so many Christians miss the joy is that they keep waiting for a time when life's complications will be resolved. We think of joy as compensation *for* working things out for the Lord. Instead, true joy is His companionship during the battle, not only after the battle. Many of us feel we have no right to feel joyous as long as we are not perfect, still have areas in which we need to grow, and continue to face unresolved tensions. But joy is for the journey, not just for the reflective moments after the journey.

The essential difference between happiness and joy is that happiness is usually circumstantial and situational. The root of the meaning of *happiness* is *hap,* meaning "chance"; the root of joy is changeless love.

When the King is in residence we then are able to fight life's battles with joy. We become "overcomers." Troublesome people and frustrating situations, pressures and challenges, disappointments and grief, heartache and sorrow will all be infused with joy, because we know that the Lord will use them all for our growth and His glory.

Joy and Honesty

Many of us deny our humanity in our search for joy. Life is run on two tracks, one of bold beliefs and the other of life's difficulties. A Christ-filled Christian can dare to bring the two together. We can be honest with ourselves and the Lord about what we are going through and feeling. Surrender is the key. When we turn over to our Lord our real world and know that He will work everything together for good, the fruit of joy is expressed in our character and countenance.

When we block the Lord from meeting our real needs, thinking we should be responsible to work those out ourselves, we try to checkmate Him from reaching us where we need Him most desperately! That has been difficult for me to learn. There is still that lingering misconception that if I were more faithful and obedient, there would be no pressing needs in my life. False!

Once I went through a confrontation with a good friend. He had some things to say that hurt deeply. Afterward, I had a bad case of the "if onlys." Do you ever get them? As long as I dealt with my feelings defensively, there was no joy. Then I was brought to my knees again. "Lord, what can I learn from this? What are You trying to tell me? I hurt, Lord, and need You very much!" Joy flooded my heart. The situation was not resolved completely, but joy returned. I knew that the One who gives each day would show the way. There were things I needed to do and say to correct the problem, but I was able to do them with joy.

The same thing has happened to me all through my life and ministry. Joy was given me as a fruit of Christ's Spirit years ago.

The sowing and harvesting of that gift have usually come in the midst of stretching challenges and soul-sized opportunities.

I write this with you in mind. Perhaps you are going through something right now that is painful and excruciating. Most of us are. There will always be problems; that is life. But there will also be more than adequate strength; that is joy. Don't wait until the crisis is over to allow yourself the delicious fruit of joy. True joy is but a prayer of surrender away. Get in touch with where you are hurting and hoping. That will be the focus of a new joy. When your energy and resources are diminished, you can count on the Lord's joy to fuel and reinforce your human spirit in all possible (and impossible!) situations. Praise the Lord for crises. They are fresh opportunities to experience His joy.

"I Will Joy—Regardless"

In preparation for writing this chapter, I did a comprehensive review of the word *joy* in Scripture. It is almost always experienced in the context of some difficulty or in reflection on what the Lord has made of the raw material of discouragement. What the Lord will do, is doing, and has done, is our joy.

The prayer of Habakkuk has become one of my favorites. It reminds us that the fruit of joy is produced when other harvests are barren.

Though the fig tree may not blossom,
Nor fruit be on the vines;
Though the labor of the olive may fail
And the fields yield no food;
Though the flock may be cut off from the fold,
And there be no herd in the stalls—
Yet I will rejoice in the LORD,
I will joy in the God of my salvation.
The LORD God is my strength;
He will make my feet like deer's feet,
And He will make me walk on my high hills.

—HABAKKUK 3:17-19

Note how the word *joy* is used as part of the future verb form of the Hebrew word. Not "I will have joy," but "I will joy"! It actually means "I will spin about with delight and adoration." A pirouette of praise. A noun becomes a verb for daily living. Not a bad commitment for all of life, "I will joy—regardless."

Another verse that gives us the distilled meaning of joy is Acts 13:52, "The disciples were filled with joy and with the Holy Spirit." They had every reason not to be. They had just lived through a hard time of rejection and persecution in Antioch of Pisidia. Note what happened just before the disciples experienced the fresh flush of joy. "The Jews stirred up the devout women and the chief men of the city, raised up persecution against Paul and Barnabas, and expelled them from their region. But they shook off the dust from their feet against them, and came to Iconium" (verses 50-51).

I like that. Joy did not depend on human success, the approval of people, or having everything go right. The disciples could press on to the next challenge. The Lord gave them joy for the next steps of His strategy.

A Family Likeness

But there is a further reason some Christians miss the joy. True joy is a part of God's nature that He wants to share with His children. It is a family characteristic. What gives God joy is the source of our joy. In fact, there is no lasting joy until we are partners with God in what He is doing in the world. According to the parabolic teaching of Jesus, God experiences joy whenever we join Him in concern for the lonely and the lost. The old gospel song says, "If you want joy, real joy, wonderful joy, let Jesus come into your heart." That is fine as far as it goes. We also should sing, "If you want to keep joy, real joy, wonderful joy, let Jesus flow out of your heart to others."

Lost and Found

In the parables of the lost son, the lost sheep, and the lost coin, Jesus tells us that God and the whole company of heaven experience sublime joy whenever the lost are found. The elder brother missed sharing that joy. The shepherd who left the ninety-nine sheep in search of the one lost sheep shared the heart of God when he recovered the wandering one. And the woman who would not give up until she had found the lost coin tasted the joy of heaven when she found it. The "lost and found" department of heaven is always open.

God's joy is the result of love received. He knows no greater joy than when we let Him love us. And our joy is a by-product of allowing Him to love others through us. A personal note: The only greater joy for me than becoming a Christian has been helping other people live forever by introducing them to Christ and salvation. Joy breaks forth in inner delight when I have been given the privilege of leading another person to the Lord and to the great adventure of life in the Lord. Joy becomes a lasting fruit when I am free to love and care, give and forgive, listen to and hope for people.

Whenever Christians tell me they have lost the joy they once had, my first question is, "When was the last time you helped someone meet Christ?" How would you answer that? Who is alive in Christ because of you?

The more I study the parable of the talents in Matthew 25:14-30, the more convinced I become that Jesus was talking about reproducing our faith, enabling others to know Him. He taught the parable at the end of His ministry. He knew He was going away, the cross was ahead, and He would be back.

The parable of the talents was based on a custom of the time. Local provincial leaders deployed by the Roman Empire were often called back to Rome. While they were gone, they entrusted their properties and investments to subordinates. Jesus built on the familiar to teach an unfamiliar, and very surprising, truth. We will get the full impact if we identify the "man" going away on a journey with the Lord Himself, and the servants with the disciples and with us.

You know the story. One was given one talent, another two, and another five. Remember, a talent was worth about $1000. Whether $1000, $2000, or $5000, each was given a great sum to invest. Both the two- and five-talent servants doubled their investment. The one-talent servant was afraid of losing what he had and buried his talent in the ground.

Inevitably, the time of accounting came. Note that the two- and five-talent servants received accolades for the multiplication of their investment and were invited to a very special privilege—the *joy* of the master. The one-talent servant said, "I was afraid, and I went and hid your talent in the ground." The punishment for that was severe:

> Take the talent from him, and give it to him who has the ten talents. For to everyone who has, more will be given, and he will have abundance; but from him who does not have, even what he has will be taken away (Matthew 25:28-29).

The key to understanding the parable is in what Jesus

meant by the talent. What is the one thing He promised to entrust to us? The abundant life. And He wants to know what we have done with it. For us, the point is very clear. Those who multiply the gift of new life in Him enter into His joy. There is one kind of joy we receive in companionship with the Lord in prayer. There is an even greater joy which comes to us in adventuring with Him in involvement with people. To "enter into the joy of the Master" (with a capital M), is to share

An act of extending love, or of telling another what Christ can do with a life surrendered to Him, explodes into joy!

with others what He means to us. Whatever word you attach to it—soul-winning, sharing the faith, evangelism—matters little if the passion of our lives is bringing people to the Lord. We cannot experience deeper joy, or keep it, until we share the love we have received.

Some people are too busy for that. We refuse to be interrupted by people who are put on our agendas by the Lord. Many of us do not want a life where plans are apt to be canceled for situations of unscheduled human need. There is little place or time for sudden, unrepeatable opportunities to incarnate an act of divine love. We get hung up on what we perceive as our own spiritual maturity, a petulant perfectionism over theological details, or do's and don'ts which have little to do with Christ's purpose for us. An act of extending love, or of telling another what Christ can do with a life surrendered to Him, explodes into joy!

Needy candidates for Christ's love are all around us. Love-starved people are everywhere. Unblessed children of loveless marriages. Distraught parents. People locked into the syndrome of sameness. Friends who are anxious and worried. Associates who are missing the reason they were born. Neighbors tied down like Gulliver to the accumulation of things, and acquaintances who are more ready to talk about their heartaches than we are to listen. Some of those people will not know joy now and may not live forever because we hid the talent of our abundant life in the ground.

◄ ─ ◄━◄◆►━► ─ ►

Have I written myself into a contradiction? How can the fruit of Christ's joy be freely given and yet depend so much on our response? All I have tried to say is that which we will not use, we lose. Joy is ours as a result of grace. But it is for the realities of life. And it lasts as long as it is given away.

Robert Louis Stevenson was right: "To miss the joy is to miss all."

Within You to
Give You Peace

Peace is not only a gift of Christ, it is Christ
Himself living His life in us.

I am going to ask you some very personal questions. Audacious? Maybe. But if you and I could sit down and talk together over a cup of coffee, these are the questions I would ask
you—and I would like you to ask me:

- What is it that robs you of peace?

- Who is it in your life who hassles you to the point where
  you lose your inner calm—that sense of unity and peace?

- What is it in your life that makes you impatient and
  stretches your innermost self to the place of breaking?

- Who is it who can rankle you to the place that you lose

your countenance and blast that person for what he or she is or has done?

We all have a breaking point, a place where life gets to us, when it seems impossible to feel peace or express patience. Here the fallacy hits us once again. We have been taught all our lives that peace was something we could condition by thinking the right thoughts.

There is nothing wrong with good mental hygiene, but the peace that will see us through the deep turbulence of our times is not programmed mind-control. Such peace cannot be induced by drugs or patched into the fabric of our tissues like an electrode.

Peace is the pearl we would give fortunes for. "Peace," Matthew Henry said, "is such a precious jewel that I would give anything for it but truth."

The fruit of Christ's indwelling Spirit is peace.

Longing for Peace

Our mental institutions are filled with people longing for peace. Walk along any street in any city in America. We can all see the expressions on the faces of people that indicate a lack of peace in their hearts.

Is it any wonder the word *peace* was so often on the lips of our Lord? He greeted His disciples with the single word, "Peace!" The early church was characterized by the greeting,

"The peace of the Lord Jesus be with you!" A part of the historic Eucharist has been *pax tibiti*—"Peace to you!"

In Hebrew the word for "peace" is *shalom*. In Greek it is *eirēnē*. In Latin it is *pax*. What is this peace?

Peace is more than a state of freedom from hostility, more than harmony or a temporary truce in personal relationships. We need to plumb deeply into the nature of the peace our Lord had in mind when He said, "Peace I leave with you, My peace I give to you; not as the world gives do I give to you. Let not your heart be troubled, neither let it be afraid" (John 14:27).

Christ gives peace to us by virtue of His indwelling presence, the presence Paul spoke of as fruit to imply a process of growth, or degrees of development depending on our cooperation. The fruit of peace becomes resplendent in us when our acceptance of the Lord's forgiveness is complete in every level of our being.

There are memories that lurk within us and rob us of peace, memories that rub the conscience raw. When we are quiet, a familiar piece of music, or a face we have not seen for a long time, floods back into our minds and hearts, bringing with it the realization of unresolved failure, sin, or rebellion. And our peace is gone.

Our peace is also shattered when we refuse to be the agent of forgiveness in the lives of other people. Is there anyone you need to forgive, anyone who has failed you at some point in your life—in your family, the church, or in our society? Very often we carry the burden of the hurt and resentment and actually live as though Christ had not made a once, never-to-be-repeated, substitutionary reconciliation for the sin of the world in His body on the cross:

> It pleased the Father that in Him all the fullness should dwell, and by Him to reconcile all things to Himself, by Him, whether things on earth or things in heaven, having made peace through the blood of His cross (Colossians 1:19-20).

We either accept or try to reproduce that magnificent atonement. And very often we fail to forgive all. We take the burden of some failure in another person's life and carry it inside ourselves. We do it at the cost of trying to reproduce what was done at Calvary on our behalf. "A great many people are trying to make peace," D.L. Moody said, "but that has already been done. God has not left it for us to do; all we have to do is to enter into it."

Second place is the only place Christ will not take. He was rather severe about the nature of the peace He would offer when He said, "Do not think that I came to bring peace on earth. I did not come to bring peace but a sword" (Matthew 10:34). Suddenly our minds are awake to discover the kind of severing He meant:

> He who loves father or mother more than Me is not worthy of Me. And he who loves son or daughter more than

Me is not worthy of Me…He who finds his life will lose it, and he who loses his life for My sake will find it (Matthew 10:37,39).

A lack of peace is a warning signal, a jarring alarm inside us telling us that someone or something may have taken Christ's place as Lord of our hearts. Who is it? What is it? Where is it for you?

We all long to be quiet inside, to have an inner unity and oneness. The loss of this peace is the price we pay for a secondary loyalty. Jesus Christ said we cannot possibly serve two masters.

Do You Have Peace?

Are you at peace right now? Is there within you that quiet, healing distillation that only the Lord can give? The meaning of the word *peace* in Greek is the knitting-together, the unification of what has been broken and unraveled and disrupted. It means wholeness. In fact, in Hebrew, it's almost a synonym for the meaning of *salvation,* which means deliverance, oneness, wholeness, and unification.

Do I have peace? It is only fair that you should ask me that question, too. I find that though I spend my life studying the Scriptures, preaching and writing, caring for people, and getting more than my share of love and affirmation from these relationships, there are times when I feel an absence of peace. Sometimes—for a moment or day, I take my eyes off

Jesus Christ and put them on some cause or some purpose or some thing that I willfully want to do. That's when I begin to feel what I have come to call "jangledness" inside; I have to be still and go back to prayer and say, "Lord, what is it that has taken priority over You?"

A Mind Stayed on God

Do you remember that marvelously clean and uncluttered sentence written by the prophet Isaiah on this very subject?

The third and fourth verses of Isaiah 26 command attention not just because they are familiar but because they give us secrets to lasting peace. "You will keep him in perfect peace, whose mind is stayed on You, because he trusts in You. Trust in the LORD forever, for in YAH, the LORD, is everlasting strength."

The English words of verse 3 have been a cherished promise for God's peace through the centuries. "You will keep him in perfect peace." At first we're tempted to get at the meaning of the quality of peace God offers by defining the word *perfect*. We say that *perfect peace* is "complete peace, peace that is found in tranquil surroundings and with agreeable people." But this only touches the outskirts of what Isaiah meant.

The word *perfect* is not in the Hebrew text. Rather the word for "peace," *shalom,* is repeated twice: *shalom, shalom*— like "holy, holy." Alec Motyer calls this a "super-superlative."

"This is unlike other super-superlatives in the Bible," according to my friend Rabbi Yechiel Eckstein, the founder and president of the International Fellowship of Christians and Jews. "In this instance, the second use of the word *shalom* is not so much for emphasis as it is for definition and interpretation. For example, we might say, 'John is a fine man, fine in the sense that he is good to his children.' This can be proven by the fact that in the Hebrew text there is a vertical line between the two words of *shalom* to show precisely this idea: *shalom|shalom.*"

This idiom of duplication distinguishes pseudo-peace from God's peace, which is total peace encompassing all dimensions of the mind, emotion, will, and body as well as relationships, sense of righteousness, and perception of justice for living.

The first step to this kind of peace, according to Isaiah, is to stay our minds on God. "You will keep him in *shalom, shalom,* whose mind is stayed on You."

The Hebrew word for "mind" used here is *yēser.* It means "the constitution or tendency of the mind," what we might call a "frame of mind" or a "mind-set"—a total way of looking at things. Another way of putting it would be the "focus of our attention" or "what we have on our minds most of the time." *Yēser* corresponds closely to the Greek word *phroneite* as used in Philippians 2:5: "*Let this mind be* in you which was also in Christ Jesus." Precisely translated, it means, "Let this be your attitude."

J.N. Oswalt points out in his commentary on Isaiah,

> As a noun *yēṣer* frequently refers to that which is formed, often thoughts, purposes, or intentions. As reflected in the present translation, the Hebrew seems to place "the steadfast mind" in an emphatic position in an independent clause at the beginning of the sentence.

Practically, this means that God's superlative peace is given to those whose minds are intentionally riveted on Him.

A Mind Stayed on God

We must keep our minds stayed on God. The Hebrew word for "stayed" is *samúk*. The wonderful thing is that *samúk* is a passive participle. It's something God does. He stays our minds on Him. As we start the day, we need only say, *Lord, I belong to You. I've been called out of this world to glorify You, to experience Your love and forgiveness, and to know peace in spite of what's going on around me. Now, Lord, I ask You for what You are more ready to give than I am willing to receive. Stay me, Lord. Stay me on Yourself. Interrupt me. Stop me. Permeate my thoughts. Call me back to You. Keep me stayed on You.*

And He'll do it. If your mind wanders off, then it wanders off to a place that Christ wants you to deal with. Don't worry about a wandering mind. Just follow the wandering, and you'll end up someplace where the Lord wants you to deal with an issue, a relationship, a concern, a problem. Too many people complain, "I begin to pray, and my mind wanders off." I say, "Wonderful! Let it wander and then bring Christ with you, and if you bring Him into your wandering, you'll soon find out the thing that's keeping you from Him."

What a great assurance! You can go to work tomorrow morning knowing that the Lord is not going to let you get Him off your mind. He's not going to let you, because you belong to Him.

And what about the rest of the day? Do you have to become a victim of people and circumstances? Definitely not! The one confidence nothing and no one can take from you is your ability to pray without ceasing. The shams of life may rage around you, but inside there will be calm because you can pray your way through it all. You can pray in the midst of uncertainties, conflict, turmoil, and adversity. Prayer will stay your mind on Christ and fill your thoughts with His peace. You can pray before, during, and after challenging conversations with people. You can claim peace when you are in the most alarming, disquieting situations.

You also need to allow Christ to stay your mind on the good things. Peace and praise go together. There's a renewed, fresh gift of peace in gratitude. Think about the Lord's signature in the beauty of the natural world, the way He works out solutions to your needs, the wondrous gift of people He uses to help you, and the open doors of opportunity He sets before you. What a wonderful way to live!

A Mind Stayed on the Kingdom

Jesus challenged His disciples—and He challenges us—to seek first the kingdom of God. I like the way the New English version of the Bible translates this verse, Matthew 6:33: "Set your mind on God's kingdom...before everything else."

The kingdom of God is His sovereignty in action, His reign and rule over everything. So, setting your mind on the kingdom is the same thing as staying your mind on the rule of God. There is no peace apart from seeking to know and to do God's will. Through the guidance of Christ, we are also given specific direction. I'm convinced that Christ does speak to our hearts; we are given "words of knowledge" about situations and people and we can hear them if we listen attentively. A mind that Christ stays on God—sets on the kingdom—is a mind with spiritual eyes to see and perceptive ears to hear.

We cannot be at peace if we have been given marching orders in a particular relationship or sector of our lives and refuse to follow them. Once we say, "Lord, what do *You* want me to do? What do *You* want me to say? How do *You* want me to act?" and consciously refuse to follow the clear directive He gives, we will not know peace. Faithful obedience—that is the environment that develops the fruit of peace.

Paul used an athletic term to help the Colossian Christians understand how the peace factor enables us to know what is creative for us, and what could be debilitating. He advised, "Let the peace of Christ rule in your hearts" (3:15 NIV). The Greek word for "rule" means *umpire*. The indwelling Christ will call the plays—*safe* or *out*.

The apostle also spoke of peace as a protector. Listen to this:

> Be anxious for nothing, but in everything, by prayer and supplication, with thanksgiving, let your requests be made known to God; and the peace of God, which surpasses all understanding, will guard your hearts and minds through Christ Jesus (Philippians 4:6-7).

The word for "guard" in the phrase "guard your hearts and minds" means to garrison, to watch out for, to stand as a sentinel. Paul uses a military word in Greek—*phrourein,* "standing on guard." Christ's Spirit is within us on round-the-clock duty, guarding, watching for approaching danger, sounding the warning-signal, defending us from all that would produce panic in our hearts. When we trust Him, there is peace.

Making Peace with Others

It is one thing to have peace, to savor peace, to be managed and protected by this divine implant of Christ. But there is one thing more: You can be the Lord's agent in making peace for others. "Blessed are the peacemakers," Jesus said, "for they shall be called sons of God" (Matthew 5:9). The dividends from such an investment of yourself have no equal. To be a peacemaker means to be actively involved with God in the task of reconciling people to Himself.

If we want Christ's peace in our hearts, we must be engaged in combating negative criticism, gossip, and innuendos that destroy relationships.

The fruit of peace bears fruit. The fruit of one Christian is another. We are to be reproductive. Our Christian life is not complete until we become active, contagious communicators of Christ's love to others. Each of us was introduced to the Savior by someone who cared enough to become involved in listening and loving. I would not be writing this book if it had not been that two college friends took time to earn the right to show me that my emptiness was a longing for purpose and power that only Christ could give. I saw the peace of Christ in them and wanted what they had.

We cannot make peace by ourselves. It is Christ-grown. But each of us can be His agent in "making" peace with others. That means taking the initiative: being the first to ask for or express forgiveness and restitution.

Each of us can also be Christ's special agent in reconciling people to each other, as an unassuming, "unofficial" peace presence in the tensions that explode around us. We are to listen to both sides without taking sides. We can go to people who are separated in conflict and misunderstanding. Our task is to open the channels of understanding and empathy. Often it is necessary to help people pray for forgiveness and the power to be forgiving.

Whenever we get in touch with the anguish in people or whenever we identify our own struggles, we realize how much we need the peace of Christ and how much we need to become peacemakers. His Spirit of peace in us can make all the difference.

Peace flows into us when we allow it to flow out of us in active peacemaking. Today is the time for initiating peace. Anything which keeps people apart is our concern and responsibility as peacemakers. If we want Christ's peace in our hearts, we must be engaged in combating negative criticism, gossip, and innuendos that destroy relationships. Our constant concern will be to help people forgive, accept, and understand one another. Think of what life could be if our purpose were to bring reconciliation among our families and friends!

Here is a daily motto. Put it on your desk, on the wall of your kitchen, or beside your bed to read when you start each day.

God was in Christ reconciling the world to himself, not counting their trespasses against them, and entrusting to us the message of reconciliation. So we are ambassadors for Christ, God making his appeal through us (2 Corinthians 5:19-20 RSV).

Peace is not only a gift of Christ, it is Christ Himself living His life in us, His presence in our hearts and minds. It is abiding in Christ and allowing Him to abide in us.

Our Lord gives us the gift to be able to picture what we would be like if His peace dwelt in our hearts. Imagine yourself as a peace-possessed person. Now picture the peace of Christ's love and forgiveness flowing among all your loved ones and friends.

Prayer for peace comes from a lively, Christ-inspired imagination. Once we have the picture, we can ask Christ to give us His legacy of peace. He is more ready to give than we are to ask. Praying for peace begins with Him. He motivates us to ask for what He has prepared for us through His life, the cross, an empty tomb, and a present power. Now we can say and mean, "Peace be in you! May the peace of the living Christ live in your hearts." The fruit of Christ's Spirit is peace. It is a cherished aspect of the essence of His presence.

15

Within You to
Give You Patience

How can we be patient in an impatient world?

The fourth aspect of the character transplant the indwelling Christ can perform in us is to impute His patience. Good thing. The character trait of patience is one we all need. So I pray for you...and myself, "The Lord go within you to give you patience."

━━━━✦━━━━

The shortest moment in time occurs when you are stopped in your car at an intersection. It's the split second between the instant the traffic light turns green and when the person in the car or truck behind you leans on his horn impatiently.

This time it was no ordinary horn. The blaring blast almost lifted me off my seat. Startled, I checked my rearview mirror. A gigantic Mack truck with an ominous-looking grill was behind me. A grim-faced driver was shaking his fist. I checked the traffic light. It was just now turning green! Another fierce blast of the horn—I got moving as quickly as I could.

Not fast enough, though, for the truck driver behind me; no matter how fast I drove, I couldn't get away from him. At any moment I thought he was going to drive that motorized projection of his ego right up over the trunk of my car. Persistently he blew his imperious-sounding horn.

Finally, after being tracked down for four blocks, I pulled over to the curb and stopped my car. The truck sped past me with the driver again shaking his fist and shouting what I imagined were obscenities. Then, to my surprise, the truck swerved to the curb and parked in front of a store just ahead of where I had sought refuge.

I expected the driver to jump out of the cab of his truck and give me the unwelcome gift of a further piece of his impatient mind. Instead, he just sat there, aimlessly, as if he had nothing else to do. Apparently, his impatience had nothing to do with his delivery schedule.

I sat in my car for a moment before I drove on. I began to laugh at myself. I had been very impatient with people and situations that day. The Lord had allowed me to receive a strong dose of my own mood from this reckless, impatient truck driver.

Still chuckling to myself about the way the Lord uses situations to expose us to our impatient selves, I slowly drove my car up to the side of the truck. I rolled down the window on the passenger side and, with a thumbs-up signal, called out to the driver, "Hey, thanks for the message!"

As I drove on I thought of a wonderful retort given by a man whose car had stalled at an intersection. While the lights changed several times, a woman in the car behind him relentlessly blew her horn.

Finally, the man got out of his car and casually walked back to the woman. "Would you do me a favor?" he asked. "Please go up and try to get my car started while I sit in your car and blow the horn!"

That's the kind of clever remark we usually think about making hours after we've become impatient with someone's impatience!

Trying to Be Patient in an Impatient World

But our impatience is not limited to blowing the horns of our cars. Many of us have an inner horn we blow when things don't go our way or people get in our way. Some of us are racehorses who get perturbed by the turtles who clutter up the racetrack of life.

We live in an impatient society catered to by fast-food restaurants, products which provide instant satisfaction, and a host of businesses which offer immediate service. An experience the other day brought this into sharp focus.

I was out of town, and I needed a suit cleaned and pressed in a hurry. I found one of those "Fresh as a Flower in Just One Hour," quick-cleaning establishments. The sign on the door said, *We cater to impatient people in a hurry.* Feeling that I qualified on both counts, I presented my crumpled, well-traveled suit to the owner. He took my name and with an unpleasant attitude demanded, "When do you want it? Yesterday, I suppose!"

My first inclination was to grab my suit back and tell him he could keep his cleaning fluids and the juices of his unpleasantness to himself, but my pride got the best of me when I thought of speaking in that wrinkled suit. I pointed to the sign with all the one-hour, for-people-in-a-hurry promises. "Yeah, that's right," he said tempering his tone a bit. "It's been a hard day. I guess I'm impatient with impatient people!" We both laughed, the tension was relaxed, and he cleaned and pressed my suit…in a hurry!

As I walked back to my hotel, I reflected on the living parable I had just experienced. The very thing that shop wanted to be known for was the one thing the proprietor was tired of producing. He wanted to serve impatient people and yet his impatience bristled when asked to do what the sign promised.

Then it hit me: I would like to be known as a patient person. I preach about it, try to help others discover it, and yet I find impatience a difficult problem to conquer. I had never met the cleaning man before, and yet his diagnosis was on target: I do like to have everything yesterday!

How about you? Ever troubled with impatience? Do difficult people test your patience? Does what they do or fail to do get to you? Are you ever upset when people you love fail to capture the vision you have for them? Ever get exasperated when people do not meet your expectations of what you want them to accomplish on your time schedule? And more profoundly, knowing people's potential and what the Lord can do with a life given over to His control, do you become impatient with their slow response or imperviousness?

And what about the problems in our society and the world? Does reading the newspaper or watching the news fill you with indignation? With all our scientific advancement and technological skill, we have not come very far in human progress. Or what about the slowness of political machinery? Does your blood boil over our ineptness and inefficiency in grasping and solving problems? To top it off, there is the computerized impersonalization of modern business. Have you tried to straighten out a bill you have overpaid or underpaid?

And behind it all are people whose goofs and oversights gum up the highly polished machinery. People like you and me!

Another source of our impatience is ourselves. Have you been astounded, as I have at myself, by the little progress you've made in some areas? In your personal life and attitudes? Your relationships? Your work and professional advancement? Most of us could qualify for the sign in the quick-cleaning shop. We are impatient and in a hurry. But where are we going so fast?

If we were to get where we are going, where would we be? If we acquired all that we want, what would we have? When it is all over, what is the one-word epitaph they could put on our gravestone? *Patient?* Not I, nor most of us.

But let's not be too severe with ourselves. Go deeper. Our real problem is finding the balance between a divinely inspired discontent and simply accepting ourselves and things as they are. We are thankful for the reformers, inventors, and visionaries of history who did not accept the lie that what is must always be. The people who helped history turn its crucial corners were people who had a dream and dared to stick with it. They were patient and creatively impatient all at the same time. Endurance marked their characters. They persisted with the vision until it came of age.

Perhaps our problem with *im*patience is that we misunderstand *patience*. It is not acquiescence, or perpetual placidity, or feckless lack of fiber. Patience must be rooted in an overarching confidence that there is Someone in control of this universe, our world, and our lives. We need to know that God works things together for good for those who love Him (see Romans 8:28). A patient person knows the shortness of time and the length of eternity. *Patience is faith in action.*

Impatient with God

Now we have come to the real source of our impatience: Often we are really impatient with God! Sometimes we call it the problem of unanswered prayer. Most often, it's simply that we can't get God marching to the cadence of what we want when we want it. The most frustrating word in our lexicon is *wait.* We run ahead of God in what we desire and lag behind in doing what He desires of us.

Patience is really an attribute of God. When He met Moses on Mount Sinai, God's own self-disclosure was, "The LORD, the LORD God, merciful and gracious, *longsuffering,* and abounding in goodness and truth" (Exodus 34:6). Moses used these very words when he later prayed for God's patience with Israel. The psalmist claimed God's patience when he pulled out all the stops in soaring adoration:

> Bless the LORD, O my soul; and all that is within me bless His holy name!…The LORD is merciful and gracious, *slow to anger,* and abounding in mercy (Psalm 103:1,8).

Here the Hebrew words for "slow to anger" literally mean "long in the nostrils"! The idea was that anger was vented from the nostrils—and God's patience with His people was long and enduring. The prophet Joel knew this and called Judah to "return to the Lord your God, for He is gracious and merciful, *slow to anger,* and of great kindness" (Joel 2:13).

We discover what patience *is* from God. He has all the time in the world. And He is on time with His interventions to help us, in time with His guidance and forgiveness. God's word to us about patience has been spoken in the Word, Christ Jesus. In Christ we see patience incarnate. It was a vital trait in the character He came to reveal. Living on God's timing, Christ was never in a hurry. Saturated with prayer, He sought only to know and do His Father's will. Christ's obedience led to the cross and His atoning death for our forgiveness. All so that when He rose victoriously from the grave, He could call into being a new creation of creatures in whom He could engender His own character.

True patience is a supernatural character trait. It is a part of the fruit of the Spirit given to those who believe in Christ as Savior and Lord *and* are filled with His Spirit. Patience is the mysterious fruition of love, joy, and peace.

The fruit of Christ's Spirit is patience.

Only One Person Can Teach Us to Be Patient

If we would learn patience, Christ alone can teach us. There are many facsimiles of this character trait, but authentic, lasting patience comes as a result of a deep personal relationship with Christ.

The original Greek word Paul used for patience in the list of the fruit of the Spirit is *makrothumia*. It's a compound word: *makros*—"long or far"; and *thumos*—"hot, anger, wrath or temper." Patience is long or slow anger, or long-tempered. "Temper" is a word that describes the quality of our attitudes, the characteristic frame of our minds. Another way of putting it is that attitudes are congealed thought and the expression of those attitudes comprises our temperament. We talk about quick-tempered or even-tempered people. The fruit of Christ's Spirit in us makes us *long*-tempered.

Another word for patience in the New Testament is *hupomone*. It reveals how we become long-tempered. *Hupomone* also is a compound word: *hupo*—"under"; *meno*—"to abide." When the Spirit of Christ abides in us, we abide under His control. We are enabled by Him to wait for His perspective and power. If we trust Him, He will guide us in how we are to react and what we are to say. Our temperament is transformed by Christ in us. Mysteriously, the transplant of His character trait of patience is planted in us and begins to grow. He reminds us of His unqualified love and forgiveness, His indefatigable patience with us in our failures, and His repeated interventions to help us. Christ never gives up on us. And as we abide under His gracious care, we discover a new power to be long-tempered, that is, patient, with ourselves and others.

But the wonder of it all is that He is the patience we are able to express.

❖

Christ is peace. Christ is patience. We could never produce these graces on our own strength, in the quantities that are needed in our families and our world. But we do have access to an unlimited stockpile of patience when the fruit of Christ's patience gives us courage to live on His timing and act with His power. The Lord go within you to give you...patience.

16

Within You to Help You Get Up When You're Down

May Christ go with you, filling you with His kindness,
so you can get up when you get down on yourself.

Do you ever get down on yourself? It happens to all of us at times, whenever we feel we do not measure up to our own standards. It attacks when we fail to do what we planned, or compulsively repeat old habits we thought we had left behind. Our accomplishments do not match our expectations. Dreams are unfulfilled, hopes are dashed, and agendas are tardy. Who's to blame? "I am!" we say to ourselves. Now the "if onlys" of the past invade the "what ifs" of the present. We are engulfed in a sense of guilt. "If I had been different...if I had worked harder...if I had been wiser...if I had been stronger," becomes the dirge of self-incrimination.

We all have an awesome capacity for self-scrutiny. We can analyze our own performances and personalities. Coupled with that is our capacity to remember; we are haunted by old memories of what we did that we shouldn't have done, and what we should have done that we never accomplished. That's when we become our own parent, or our own diminutive god, and take over the punishment of ourselves. Discouragement and depression result. Our conscience shakes an accusing finger.

Self-condemnation sets in. Self-esteem drains out. We begin to feel badly about ourselves. Self-negation dominates our feelings. It is then that we are the most vulnerable, and the most apt to do what we promised ourselves we would never do: We act out our depleted self-image. Others are treated the way we treat ourselves. We become unkind in word and action. Our sense of guilt thrashes about searching for something to do that will support our negative self-appraisal—all so we can say to ourselves, *See—what you did is what you are!*

It is difficult to get up for life when we are down on ourselves. What can we do about our sense of guilt, self-negation, and resultant self-condemnation? What would it take to give us a whole new picture of ourselves as loved and lovable, forgiven and forgiving?

I talked to a man who was down on himself. After he had told me all the things he could muster to support his bad feelings about himself, he said a stunning thing, "If I could only forget the failures and remember the accomplishments, I'd be okay—I've got a good memory and a poor forgetter."

Our inability to forget gives our compulsive conscience lots of accusing ammunition.

A poor forgetter! The word is not in the dictionary. It should be. Allow me to venture a definition: A "forgetter" is the capacity to forget the failures and inadequacies of the past. What we remember and what we forget is crucial for our spiritual and mental health. The only way to get up when we are down on ourselves is to have our memories healed and our forgetters strengthened.

The great French philosopher Henri Bergson said that it is the function of the brain to not only remember but to also forget. We laugh: "I must have a super brain because of all the things I forget!" Who has not forgotten someone's birthday or an important date on our calendars? We do not need training in forgetfulness. We are highly trained experts in that! But why is it that we forget things we want to remember and remember things we long to forget? Why is it that one failure sticks in our memory and hundreds of achievements are forgotten?

There are lots of self-improvement courses available for memory training, but I have never seen one on how to forget. Yet our inability to forget gives our compulsive conscience lots of accusing ammunition. We need just as much help in developing our "forgetter."

We cannot do that for ourselves. We are immobilized by feelings of guilt. Others cannot help us. They are either too down on themselves to help, or too glib in their encouraging affirmations to be taken seriously. It does not help for someone to tell us we are great if we feel gross. Their accolades are dismissed by our incriminating self. *If they only knew! They wouldn't be so magnanimous.*

Learning Self-Forgiveness

A healthy forgetter is developed by forgiveness. We cannot erase the memory entries of our failures in our brain computers until we have a profound experience of forgiveness. The authentic mark of truly mature persons is the capacity to forgive themselves. What a rare commodity! Years of experience in seeking to be a whole person and helping others with their self-esteem have led me to the conclusion that one of the greatest miracles of life is self-forgiveness. I have never known a person who has been able to do it without a healing experience of Christ's kindness.

The purpose of this chapter is to plumb the depths of self-condemnation and to show how Christ's kindness can help us get up when we are down on ourselves. His kindness *for* us enables a kindness *in* us for ourselves, and then for others.

The fruit of Christ's Spirit is kindness. May the Lord be in you to give you His kindness.

The Sheer Kindness of God

Kindness is the steadfast love of the Lord in action toward those who fail and to those in need. Throughout the Old Testament, the words for steadfast love, mercy, kindness, and loving-kindness are used interchangeably to translate the Hebrew word *hesed*. It is the covenant word that expresses God's persistent, pursuing effort to reach His chosen, called, and cherished people and enable them to return to Him. *Hesed* is one of the three attributes of His nature that God especially wants His people to know and experience.

> Let not the wise man glory in his wisdom, let not the mighty man glory in his might, let not the rich man glory in his riches; but let him who glories glory in this, that he understands and knows Me, that I am the LORD, exercising *lovingkindness,* judgment, and righteousness in the earth (Jeremiah 9:23-24).

God's kindness is His prevenient, unmotivated love at the heart of His nature, offered not because we deserve it or even because we pray long and hard enough to think we have earned it. This kindness of God is not motivated into action because of how good or bad we are. He is kind to us not because of what we've said or done. God is kind because that is His nature, and in kindness, He constantly seeks to reach us in our lost and lonely estrangement from Him.

The incarnation was the most convincing, undeniable evidence of God's kindness. God came in Christ out of sheer kindness. Jesus the Christ was kindness incarnate. He came to express it; lived to model it; died to offer it to us. He went to the cross not because people asked for a sacrifice for their sins, but because, out of kindness, God willed to redeem us. God raised Christ from the dead as a final victory over the power of death and evil and made Him reigning Lord over the church with authority to fill His followers with His kindness.

A new breed of humanity was created: women and men overwhelmed by the kindness of God in Christ. And through the indwelling of the Spirit of Christ in them, they discovered that they could now express to others the kindness they had received.

One who became the recipient of this amazing kindness of the early Christians was a Pharisee who was determined to persecute them. His name was Saul of Tarsus. Through the witness of the Christians in Damascus, the vigilant Pharisee experienced for himself the kindness of Christ. He became a new creature in Christ. His rigid hostility toward others and himself was melted by Christ's unsurpassed kindness. After 14 years of secluded prayer and study, Paul was a new man ready to spread to the then-known world the good news of the kindness of God's love and forgiveness in Christ.

This triumphant grace note in the apostle's message is expressed in Ephesians 2:4-7:

> But God, who is rich in mercy, because of His great love with which He loved us, even when we were dead in trespasses, made us alive together with Christ (by grace you have been saved), and raised us up together, and made us sit together in the heavenly places in Christ Jesus, that in the ages to come He might show the exceeding riches of His grace in His *kindness* toward us in Christ Jesus.

The Lord never demands anything from us that He is not willing to give us. It should not be surprising, then, that the power to be kind is also available under the special designation *fruit*. Paul discovered that kindness is implanted, imputed, and ingrained into the very nature of our new heredity in Christ Jesus. It is a fruit of Christ's Spirit in us, and, like love, joy, peace, and patience, it has a supernatural origin, a progressive growth and an undeniable fruition in our character. Kindness can now be expressed to ourselves and in our relationships with others.

The Greek word Paul used for kindness is *chrestotes*. When

he speaks of the kindness of God it is used as an expression of His grace. "When the kindness and the love of God our Savior toward men appeared, not by works of righteousness which we have done, but according to His mercy He saved us" (Titus 3:4). As a part of Christ's character transplant, kindness enables us to be as merciful and gracious to ourselves and others as *Christ has been to us.*

One of the best ways to understand and appropriate Christ's kindness as a quality of our new character is to reflect on how He was kind to people during His ministry. When we live in the skin of those who received His kindness, expressed in gracious forgiveness, only then can we forgive ourselves and be kind to one another.

Kindness to an Unfaithful Woman

No encounter in Scripture reveals the kindness of Christ better than the account of the woman caught in adultery (John 7:53–8:11). What happened to the woman exemplifies what occurs when the kindness of Christ penetrates the dark places of hidden memories and remorse.

Put yourself in the scene: We are there in the crowd listening to the Master teach in the precincts of the Temple. Suddenly His teaching is interrupted by the jeers and frenzied cries of a crowd that approaches. A ghastly procession breaks through the crowd around Jesus. It is led by scribes and Pharisees dragging an unresisting woman. An angry bloodthirsty mob follows close behind. They push her down before Jesus. She writhes in anguished sobs. What charge deserves this kind of treatment? It is obvious that she is no woman of the streets, no sensuous enticer of men's affections for a price. There is a dignity which has been crushed by this cruelty, a discernible longing which has been twisted and maligned.

Our hearts ache for the woman. We feel a combination of embarrassment and shock. Our own hidden thoughts and memories are jabbed awake. Who has not had fantasies and feelings, if not actual failures, which, if exposed, would put us at Jesus' feet?

We look into the fiendishly frenzied faces of the scribes and Pharisees. Condemnation oozes from their every pore. Then our eyes fall on their hands. In each one is a large stone. They are ready to stone her! What crime deserves this? But we know the answer.

The scribes and Pharisees confirm our suspicions. "Teacher!" they say, addressing Jesus in supercilious mockery of His sacred title, "This woman was caught in adultery, in the very act." Their voices grow in self-righteous intensity. "Now Moses, in the law, commanded that such should be stoned. But what do You say?" Our minds leap back to the ancient Scriptures. We think of Leviticus 20:10: "The man who commits adultery with another man's wife, he who commits adultery with his neighbor's wife, the adulterer and the adulteress, shall surely be put to death." The woman does not have a chance!

We look at her, crumpled and broken, before Jesus. How do we feel about that charge? Questions begin to surge into our minds. Where is the man, if the woman was taken in the *very* act? Wasn't he equally guilty? And how did the scribes and Pharisees find her in her adulterous act? Could it have been staged? Is it possible that one of those holding a stone enticed her into the compromising indiscretion so the leaders could present Jesus with an impossible decision? But what was it that motivated the angry condemnation of these leaders?

Suddenly it dawns on us that they would have to have been down on themselves before they could make such a vitriolic attack on this woman. There is so much more than meets the eye here. These men are more hostile toward Jesus than they are toward the woman! Could it be that He has put a finger on a raw nerve in them through His teaching and preaching? Were they convicted before they convicted the woman?

Jesus is confronted with an impossible dilemma. If He denies the Law, He might be stoned Himself. If He sanctions the execution of the woman, He will be going against Rome, which has forbidden capital punishment by the Jews and their courts. There seems to be no way out. The condemning leaders have used a human being as a thing to trap Him. Jesus has gained the reputation of being a friend to sinners. Will this force Him to deny His compassionate ministry? We watch Him closely to observe what He will do.

We are deeply moved by the look on His face, as He stares into the faces of the angry mob and then down at the woman at His feet. She is too ashamed to lift her head.

◆───≡◆≡───◆

Then, deliberately He stoops down. He lowers His head. What is He doing? The silence is alarming. We all wait with bated breath.

With majestic authority He raises His hand, His forefinger extended with royal dignity. All eyes are immediately focused on that regal finger. Will He use it to point accusingly at the woman, at the leaders, or at us? Instead, He slowly deliberately begins to write in the dusty sand of the ground. We strain our necks to see what He is writing. We cannot get close enough to discern it.

The leaders do not want to know. First one, and then another, begins to jibe and press Him in demanding tones. The crowd picks up the chant. "Give us an answer. The woman's guilty! Make your judgment!"

Jesus straightens to full height. Fire flashes from His eyes like lightning. The thunder of His voice follows quickly. It hits us like a blow. "He who is without sin among you, let him throw a stone at her first." A murmur of uneasiness grips the crowd. No one expected that. The tables have turned. Those who wanted to trap Jesus are now the ones who feel trapped.

Once again Jesus stoops to write in the sand. What is He writing? It must be convicting, whatever it is, because now the leaders suddenly have panic on their faces. They look at each other with expressions that silently speak a frightened, "How did He know?" The Lord must be writing the commandments or the hidden sins He discerned in these condemnatory leaders. Or could it be that He is writing the Hebrew word *hesed,* reminding the people of the mercy of God? Or is it the Hebrew letters for *Yahweh,* asserting that He, the Messiah, the I AM, has authority to judge and forgive?

⊢—⊨✦⊨—⊣

Silence again. No one is moving a muscle. And then the silence is broken by the thud of a large stone on the ground. We observe that the eldest of the Pharisees has dropped his stone. His judgment-worn face is twisted; now the hard lines of indignant superiority are softened a bit. Then there is another thud, and then another. The carefully selected sharp and craggy stones begin to rain down at the feet of the accusing, judgmental critics.

The woman cringes, expecting each one to hit her in judgment for her crime. She lifts her head in amazement as the leaders turn away, some in shame; others in grumbling defeat; others in retreat to find another chance to attack Jesus. We want to leave, too. Nasty business this!

We feel anguish for the woman and anxiety for ourselves. We want to get out of there before Jesus writes our hidden sins upon the ground or reminds us of our merciless attitude toward ourselves, or toward others.

We walk away hoping not to be noticed. Then, glancing back, we observe the most tender encounter we have ever seen. Jesus is still stooping. His finger in the sand. The broken woman looks up and her eyes meet His. Kindness radiates from His face. He stands up with measured movements, lifting the woman until they are face-to-face. We can hear what He says. Awesome pity and a pitiful person meet. "Woman, where are those accusers of yours? Has no one condemned you?

Do you hear His kindness in your own soul? "Neither do I condemn you. Go and sin no more!"

The woman looks around in amazement. "No one, Lord." It is as if Jesus wants to underline the fact that she is free of her accusers. But now, what about her own attitude toward herself? Will she be able to forget and make a new beginning?

Jesus' words of comfort and assurance are the most compassionate and authoritative ever spoken to anyone. We feel the impact of them as we listen. We are there in the woman's place. He takes us by the shoulders, looks deeply into our eyes and says, "Neither do I condemn you; go and sin no more."

Amazing! The sin is not condoned, but there is no condemnation. Kindness affording the power to forget.

Left to ponder what this means for us, we find ourselves in the skin of the accusers and the accused. Our unresolved guilt has caused us to act like those scribes and Pharisees more often than we want to remember. Our religion has prompted more condemnation than culpability. The more uneasy we are about our past, the more we get down on ourselves, and eventually, we become arrogant, religious prigs whose insecurity is expressed by being down on others.

But we are also forced to find ourselves at Jesus' feet, guilty as charged. No one has thrown us there. We have thrust ourselves there by our own self-condemnation. And the only hope of getting up from being down on ourselves is found in His words. Do you hear His kindness in your own soul? "Neither do I condemn you. Go and sin no more."

Ever wonder what happened to the woman and her accusers after this confrontation of the destructive power of condemnation? Did the Pharisees and scribes become kinder? Perhaps some of them realized that their own feelings of guilt under the impact of Jesus' ministry had prompted them to be severe in their judgment of the woman. We would like to think that they began a new life of kindness toward others because of Jesus' writing in the ground. But history testifies that, as a group, they never allowed the experience to affect their hearts or be expressed in their behavior. They continued with condemnation until they impaled Jesus, not only on the horns of a dilemma, but on a cross. Religious judgmentalism dies hard, and is too seldom cured.

An Inside Look

If we find ourselves among the accusers in this dramatic story, we have some painful questions to ask:

1. Do we ever escape our own self-condemnation by a critical, negative spirit to others?
2. Do we project onto others our own weary sense of guilt?
3. Do we expose and malign others for sins and failures we find in ourselves?
4. Do we hold others at a distance until they measure up?
5. Do we play God by meting out judgments and demanding that people atone to us for what they have done or been?
6. Do we seek to be as merciful and gracious to others as our Lord has been to us?

But many of us find ourselves in the woman. Not only do

we feel accused, but we accuse ourselves. Our failure may not be as obvious or easily categorized as the woman's, but what we are and have done is no less serious to our Lord.

To feel the full impact of the woman's plight and how Jesus dealt with her, we need to single out whatever it is that makes us feel down on ourselves right now. What is it for you? Whether it is great or small, it is the roadblock to healthy self-acceptance and self-esteem. Think about that as we grapple with how Jesus helps us to get up when we are down on ourselves.

Whatever the syndrome of loneliness or longing, the woman ended up more down on herself than the scribes and Pharisees could ever be. They only articulated what she already felt about herself. Their enacted exposure and judgment was nothing in comparison to what she had done to herself in her own mind. She had rendered the guilty charge on herself long before she was thrown at the feet of the Master.

The woman's own self-condemnation concerns the Lord most in this story. Once He got rid of the would-be accusers, He had to deal with the most vigilant accuser of all—the person inside the woman. Until she was as kind to herself as He was, she would not be free to live a new life. She had to change her mind about herself. Three things had to be accomplished. She needed radical forgiveness, remedial forgetfulness, and releasing freedom. And Jesus provided all three.

Radical forgiveness enables us to forgive ourselves. That

can happen only if someone with an ultimate authority forgives us. Simply to forgive ourselves without the experience of forgiveness from another does not work. Jesus Christ has the authority and the power to forgive.

We have developed a lot of fancy words for our failures: maladjustments, neuroses, complexes, need-satisfaction, or emotional sickness. But only one word defines our condition—*sin,* separation from the Lord. Our deepest need is for reconciliation and relationship with Him. We are sinners. Our actions habitually break God's law for what He meant us to be. The Ten Commandments and Jesus' great commandment to love the Lord our God with all our mind, soul, and body have not gone out of style.

Move On!

Forgiveness gives us the hope of forgetting what is behind and moving on to live. We all long for that more than anything else. It is the basis of remedial forgetfulness. We wonder what happened to the woman after she parted from the Master that day. Did she continue to condemn herself? Could she forget? Only if she could remember Jesus' words of kindness more than she remembered her sin. Robert Louis Stevenson said that it is our friends who stand between us and our self-contempt. And only Jesus can be that kind of friend who can close the door of the past and keep us from wandering furtively down the corridors of debilitating memory.

The central assurance of the Christian faith is that we are new creatures in Christ—the old can pass away, the new can come! Listen to Paul who had a great deal to haunt him, "Forgetting those things which are behind and reaching forward to those things which are ahead, I press toward the goal for the prize of the upward call of God in Christ Jesus" (Philippians 3:13-14). That is why he could say,

> Therefore, from now on, we regard no one according to the flesh [from a human point of view]. Even though we have known Christ according to the flesh, yet now we know Him thus no longer (2 Corinthians 5:16).

What the apostle meant was that he no longer thought of Christ as one man among many. "God was in Christ reconciling the world to Himself" (2 Corinthians 5:19). On that basis, we no longer regard ourselves or others from the human perspective of judgment and condemnation. We are forgiven and released to forget.

> If any one is in Christ, he is a new creation; old things have passed away; behold, all things have become new. Now all things are of God, who has reconciled us to Himself through Jesus Christ...not imputing their trespasses to them, and has committed to us the word of reconciliation (2 Corinthians 5:17-18).

And that word of reconciliation begins with our own reconciliation to ourselves. Christ has taken the sin and written "paid in full" across the ledger sheet of besetting memories.

As I stressed in a previous chapter, the same capacity of the brain which we use to remember can be used *to remember to forget.* Each time the memory of our failure invades our consciousness and attacks our peace, we can recapture the experience of the kindness of our Lord and His forgiveness.

The only memories that have any power to stalk our present thoughts are those which have never been forgiven. If you have such memories, do battle with them right now. Look them in the face, and then tell the Lord about what you did or said. He lived and died for us, and He has forgiven us. We can sing with the psalmist,

> *For as the heavens are high above the earth,*
> *So great is his steadfast mercy toward those who fear him;*
> *As far as the east is from the west,*
> *So far does he remove our transgressions from us.*

—Psalm 103:11-12 rsv

Can we dare to say, "I can't forgive myself," if our Lord who created us and saved us has said, "I forgive you"? The ultimate blasphemy and the most disastrous arrogance is to be less to ourselves than the Lord has been.

Speak to yourself now in the quiet of your own heart. Say your name. "_____, I forgive you as one forgiven by the Lord."

Freedom That Releases

Now you are ready for a releasing freedom. Jesus did more

than forgive the woman. He told her to go and sin no more. How would she accomplish that? Only if her self-condemnatory spirit had been healed by the Lord's forgiving Spirit.

Paul said, "Stand fast therefore in the liberty by which Christ has made us free, and do not be entangled again with a yoke of bondage" (Galatians 5:1). A new yoke of slavery is offered every day by life's temptations and challenges. So how can we be free?

We do what we do because of what we are inside. Until those needs are met creatively, we will continue to be constantly vulnerable. We all need a new image of ourselves: Christ's picture of us—a portrait of a loved and accepted person. Until His love possesses and pervades us, we will seek to use people and things as substitutes.

The sure test that we have accepted the Lord's image of us as forgiven is that we begin to feel good about ourselves. A new dignity and self-worth will replace the negative self-depreciation. Self-hate is the prelude to all the things we do that cause us to negate ourselves.

The formula works. Allow Christ to love you; dare to love yourself as an accepted, forgiven person. He is more concerned about our reclamation than recrimination!

Now is the only moment we have. It is the first moment of our new future. Start where you stand!

There is a lovely story of a man who asked an older man in a little village what the seemingly insignificant wide place in the road was known for. "Young man," the villager responded, "this is the starting place for any place in the world. You can start from here and go anywhere you want to go."

The Fruit of Christ's Kindness

In a way, that is what Jesus Christ says to us right now. Feel His strong arms lift you up when you are down on yourself. "Neither do I condemn you. Go and sin no more!" That is all we need to know. We are forgiven, free to forget, and released to live without self-condemnation. The fruit of the kindness of the Lord will be manifested in kindness to others.

Étienne de Grellet said, "I expect to pass through life but once. If, therefore, there is any kindness I can show, or any good thing I can do to my fellow-beings, let me do it now and not defer it, as I shall not pass this way again."

One of the most effective ways to nurture the growth of the fruit of kindness, true graciousness, is to take a prolonged time for quiet reflection with pen and paper in hand. Draw a line down the center of the page. On the left side list the times the Lord forgave you and gave you the power to forgive yourself. When you finish this list take time to praise Him for all the undeserved grace you have received.

Now on the right side of your sheet of paper list the people to whom you need to express kindness in gracious forgiveness. Be specific. Put down the hurts, the slights and oversights, the painful memories that fester inside you. Whose forgiveness do you need to receive? Whom do you need to forgive?

It's helpful to keep this inventory sheet handy. When you have acted out your forgiveness, put a check beside the items on the right side of the page. When all have been done, burn the sheet. You are free!

May the indwelling kindness of Christ go in you!

17

Within You to Give You What It Takes

When we yield to the growth of Christ's imputed goodness, we really will have what it takes.

A few years ago I conducted a funeral of a very outstanding man. After the service, I accompanied the family to the cemetery. The hearse pulled up near the grave, and I took my place with the pallbearers to lead the procession. As we moved along the pathway through the gravestones, I was deeply engrossed in my memories of the man whose body we were about to bury. I felt the loss of this man who expressed the goodness of God in his life.

Reflecting on this, I was shocked by the arrogant words of an old tombstone beside the path. It marked the grave of a man buried years before. I almost stopped in my tracks. What kind of man would have that kind of a gravestone, with this kind of an epitaph? Chiseled in granite were these words: "Here lies a man who had what it takes."

What it takes for what? To live a full and abundant life? To be a success? To be powerful? To live a rich and creative life that makes a difference? To be a good person? Did God agree that the man represented by that gravestone had exemplified what it takes?

I talked to a woman who was deeply depressed. She had a very difficult life. Her husband had left her and later came back for a weekend. During the visit he secretly packed the children's clothes, and when she was away at the grocery store, he took the children. She had no way of knowing where they were. She looked at me with tears streaming down her face and said, "Lloyd, I just don't have what it takes!"

A man wrote to me about an awesome challenge he had been given. The opportunity was immense. He felt inadequate and insecure. In the letter he confessed, "If only I were good enough and had what it takes!"

⋅⋅⋅—⋅⋙⋅✦⋅⋘—⋅⋅⋅

If we are to have what it takes, it will mean that we allow Christ to work His very nature into the fabric of our character. It is His plan to do this. He is ready to implant His Spirit into the very substance of our personalities. We have discussed the resulting character traits of love, joy, peace, patience, kindness. We are now ready to talk about goodness.

The fruit of Christ's Spirit is goodness.

Without goodness we cannot have what it takes to please God or to accomplish our purpose in being alive. Goodness is the secret of really succeeding in life.

But what is goodness?

The Word Everyone Uses and No One Defines

We'd agree with nineteenth-century preacher Henry Ward Beecher, who said, "Goodness is a very composite word that everybody uses and nobody defines."

We exclaim, "Oh, for goodness' sake!" as a kind of thoughtless expression in response to things both glad and sad. At Christmastime, children are tunefully challenged to be "good for goodness' sake." We would be hard-pressed to answer if a child asked, "What's goodness?" Our answer would probably focus on the child's behavior and obedience. Most people's notion of goodness is related to agreeable behavior or flawless morality. God's idea of goodness is concerned with something much more than that.

Goodness Is the Generosity God Defines in His Son

If we would understand goodness we must look to the

nature of Christ. Goodness is a metonym for Him, one of the attributes that often serves as one of His names.

We go back to Mount Sinai to listen to what God has said about Himself. Moses pled with God, "Please show me Your glory." God's answer was, "I will make all My goodness pass before you, and I will proclaim the name of the Lord before you. I will be gracious to whom I will be gracious, and I will have compassion on whom I will have compassion" (Exodus 33:18-19).

Nothing is complicated about the use of the word good *in the Hebrew text. It means that all of the aspects of creation are ready to fulfill their purpose...to function as they were intended.*

There, for openers, is the essence of goodness: It is synonymous with God's glory, the manifestation of His presence in out rushing, generous love poured out in graciousness and compassion. When we attest that God is good, we affirm that He is always consistent, never changes, constantly fulfills His purpose, and is totally dependable. We sing with Thomas Chisholm, "O God my Father, there is no shadow of turning with Thee; Thou changest not; Thy compassions, they fail not; as Thou hast been, Thou forever wilt be."

Goodness Manifested by God

When God created the world and all aspects of it, He reviewed His work and concluded, "It is good." At the end of the sixth day of creation, He formed a human being, and then He said, "It is very good."

Nothing is complicated about the use of the word *good* in the Hebrew text. It means that all of the aspects of creation are ready to fulfill their purpose. The plant life, the seas, the fish that swim in the seas, the animals that roam the plains, and the sublime level of His creation, human beings, are all able to function as they were intended. All are good.

Now all of creation is to be a glory to God and a manifestation of His goodness to fulfill His purpose. Our essential purpose is to glorify God and to enjoy Him forever. Insofar as "all creatures great and small" keep a life consistent with the basic reason for which they exist, goodness is maintained.

We all know too well what happened, but Adam and Eve did not lose their "good" rating just because they did a lot of bad things. Evil entered their hearts. They envied God's control over them. They wanted to control their own lives and did so by refusing to be faithful to the conditions of obedience; they denied their goodness in rebellion against God.

But God did not cease to be good. He brooded over His flawed creation. The biblical account of history reveals Him persistently seeking to bring humankind back to what He had intended—good, open to Him, obedient to His guidance, trusting in His faithfulness, generous. And good people stand out on the pages of Genesis—Enoch, Noah, Abraham, Isaac, Jacob, and Joseph—all good because they eventually fulfilled their purpose of glorifying God and obeying His will in spite of their initial resistance.

Then God made one of His many big moves. He elected Moses to be the liberator, and He led His people out of Egypt, revealing His goodness in graciousness and compassion. The Commandments were graciously given to guide His people in goodness, in fulfilling their purpose in being faithful and obedient to Him.

The goodness of God was expressed in His magnificent generosity to His people. Each time the word *goodness* is used for God in the biblical accounts of His blessings on Israel, it flashes with praise for His tremendous generosity.

God's Goodness Adored

David could not contain his adoration for God's goodness. Psalm 27 records his prayer in the midst of difficult circumstances. His enemies were all around him. Those circumstantial facts, however, were quite secondary in David's focus. "I would have lost heart, unless I had believed that I would see the goodness of the Lord in the land of the living" (verse 13).

That led to the confident trust we noted earlier. "Wait on the Lord; be of good courage, and He shall strengthen your heart; wait, I say, on the Lord!" (verse 14). As we noted earlier, David trusted his divine rear guard, "Surely *goodness* and mercy shall follow me all the days of my life" (Psalm 23:6).

He was confident that "the goodness of God endures continually" (Psalm 52:1).

Perhaps one of the greatest passages in the Old Testament recounting the goodness of God is Psalm 107. The frequent repetition of the words "Oh, that men would give thanks to the LORD for His goodness" stirs our minds to think magnificently about God's generosity. If you were to write a psalm of praise for His generosity, what would you list as evidences of His goodness to you? Surely your praise would include the most awesome expression of His goodness. It's not in the list of wonderful works in Psalm 107. The prophets longed for it and predicted it with awesome precision.

The Ultimate Expression of God's Goodness

God's goodness, the ultimate expression of His generosity, was that at a time when humankind deserved it the least, He came in Jesus Christ to reveal His goodness incarnate and to die for the sins of the whole race. The glory of God, consummate goodness, stunning generosity, was revealed on Calvary. *He came to give us what it takes—to make men and women like us good from the inside.*

Goodness is an inside story. We are made good not by our efforts but by the efficacy of the atonement accomplished by Jesus Christ on the cross. Our status before God is in and through Christ. He accepts us as new creatures, made good on

Golgotha. We could not dare to come to God apart from the imputed goodness of our standing mediated through the Savior. The Lord looks at us through the focused lens of Calvary. Our confidence is not in our human facsimiles of goodness, but in our relationship with Christ. We are freed from compulsive efforts to be good enough to deserve love. Instead, we can live in the settled security of God's generosity, manifested in the goodness of Christ.

Paul confronts this issue in Romans, chapter 3. He quotes portions of Psalm 14 and 53 in establishing what we are like apart from Christ: "There is none righteous, no, not one; there is none who understands; there is none who seeks after God. They have all turned aside…There is none who does good, no, not one" (Romans 3:10-12). The apostle goes on to assert that no one will be justified, made good, by works. Then he thunders the essential truth:

> But now the righteousness of God apart from the law is revealed…even the righteousness of God, through faith in Jesus Christ, to all and on all who believe (Romans 3:21-22).

Goodness Is a Gift

To be sure we get the point that our goodness is in Christ, Paul restates the case:

> There is no difference; for all have sinned and fall short of the glory of God, being justified freely by His grace through the redemption that is in Christ Jesus, whom God set forth

as a propitiation by His blood, through faith, to demonstrate His righteousness, because in His forbearance God had passed over the sins that were previously committed, to demonstrate at the present time His righteousness, that He might be just and the justifier of the one who has faith in Jesus (Romans 3:22-26).

Our goodness in Christ is a gift. We accept it by faith and then are released to live in the flow of His goodness—to and through us. And that is possible because our life will be guided by Christ in each situation and relationship.

I appeal to you therefore, brethren, by the mercies of God, to present your bodies as a living sacrifice, holy and acceptable to God, which is your spiritual worship. Do not be conformed to this world but be transformed by the renewal of your mind, that you may prove what is the will of God, what is good and acceptable and perfect (Romans 12:1-2 RSV).

On the basis of that we can respond to Paul's challenge to "overcome evil with good" (Romans 12:21).

After we have worked through the concept of goodness as a gift accepted by faith, so many of Paul's admonitions come alive with fresh impact. Based on the fruit of goodness through our redemption and Christ's Spirit in us, we can...

- be "of good courage" (2 Corinthians 5:8)
- know that we were re-created in Christ "for good works" (Ephesians 2:10)

- render service with "good will" (Ephesians 6:7)
- bear fruit in "every good work" (2 Corinthians 9:8)
- "hold fast what is good" (1 Thessalonians 5:21)
- have a "good conscience" (1 Timothy 1:5)
- be a "good minister of Christ" (1 Timothy 4:6)
- "fight the good fight of the faith" (1 Timothy 6:12)
- be "equipped for every good work" (2 Timothy 3:17).

All the good things we should do and say will flow from the headwaters of Christ's goodness in us. We will have what Whitehead called a "habitual vision of greatness."

The Lord gets inside of us. He takes the tangled mess of our memories of what we have done or said that we never should have done or said. And He takes all the confused relationships, the fantasies and the fears, and He forgives them. He deals redemptively with our guilt and cleanses and heals us because He is good—and He created us to be good.

So our notion that goodness is obtained by a pietistic withdrawal from ungodly persons for fear of contamination is false. Our admonitions to people, "Try and be good," and eulogies like, "Here was a really good person," are comforting but usually wide of the mark of true goodness. Christ-imputed goodness can be attributed only to someone who trusts Him and is filled with His Spirit, to someone who dares in all things to trust His direction, guidance, and the impartation of His own nature.

"A Goodness Time"

Often, I'm awakened early in the morning with the people challenges of the day ahead on my mind and heart. I know that I will not have what it will take to have a maximum day without the implanted fruit of goodness, the imparted gift of knowledge, and the inspired ability to help people focus in their minds what they can be with the Lord's power. What I do know from experience is that the Lord can give me what it takes.

So, I get out of bed and begin what I call "a goodness time." It starts with a review of the Scriptures about the goodness of the Lord. Some of those I have quoted in this chapter have been memorized through the years, so I say them or sing them out loud. Then I list the recent evidences of the Lord's goodness in my life. After that, I reclaim the fruit of Christ's character, particularly the quality of goodness and the gift of knowledge. While I'm doing that I sing the words of the chorus, "God is so good, God is so good, He's so good to me." At this point, I pray individually for my family, each of the people I will encounter that day, those on my appointment calendar and others the Lord will add in the surprises of the day. I ask for the flow of His goodness through me perfectly mingled with knowledge and the sensitivity to speak the truth in love.

My best days begin with this kind of quiet time with the Lord. And—you guessed it—my least effective days are those when I don't have what it takes because I didn't take time to open the floodgate of my heart to the inrush and outflow of the goodness of the Lord.

Robert Louis Stevenson said, "There is an idea abroad among moral people that they should make their neighbors good. One person I have to make good: myself." I agree with the great Scot that we can't make people good—only the Lord can do that. But I disagree with the notion that we can make ourselves good. When we can yield to the growth of the fruit of goodness, we can have what it takes.

The Scots authors of the Westminster Shorter Catechism put it this way: "God is a Spirit, infinite, eternal, and unchangeable, in His being [in His essential nature], wisdom, power, holiness, justice, goodness, and truth."

It is possible to treasure such a profound declaration to the point where it becomes a revered document instead of a truth to be realized and appropriated. *Christ wants to make us like Himself.* That's the triumphant theme of this book. When He takes up residence in us, He makes us consistent, authentic, real persons. We become good and are able to see the right and do it, motivated by His love. We sense the needs of others, and without being told, we respond with mercy.

Christ has been good to us so that we may be good people. His goodness within us is constant. Even now, in the quiet, do you feel it? Do you sense it? Have you ever thought of the wonder of being shaped in the image of the goodness of Christ? He longs to live His life, develop His character, and love His world through you. Inadvertently, winsomely, naturally, freely—His goodness will grow in us and become part of our own character. Hugh Latimer was right: "We must first be made good before we can do good." Goodness is not just what we do but the inward good person we become through the reconciliation of the cross and the infilling of the fruit of the Spirit.

I am gratified that after I passed by the "Here lies a man who had what it takes" tombstone, I led the procession on to the open grave of the dear friend I was burying that day. We committed his body to the ground with the full assurance that he was alive in the house of the Lord. When the grave was closed, his marker was put in place. It gave his name, the years of his physical life on earth, and these powerful words, "To God be the glory." That is all any good person ever needs to say.

Through the fruit of goodness, we will *have what it takes*— for now and eternity.

18

Within You to Release
His Amazing Resources

*Faithfulness is imputed in us so we can be courageous
intercessors for Christ's very best in others.*

It's time for a recap. In the past six chapters, we have been
discussing a magnificent, mind-reorienting, future-changing
truth. Peter states it in his second letter: We are "partakers
of the divine nature" (2 Peter 1:4). We are saying that to be
a Christian is not only to believe in Christ and try to follow
Him. It also means that the attributes of His nature are created in us to be manifested through our personalities. What I
need every hour and what some of you may need as you read
this—more than you need to take your next breath—is the

knowledge that Christ is faithful, and He can give us faith that eneables true faithfulness.

The fruit of Christ's Spirit is faithfulness.

———— ✦ ————

Faithfulness is living expectantly on the amazing resources of Christ. That means prayer. Since most of our needs have to do with people, it means intercessory prayer. The fruit of faithfulness is expressed in consistent prayer for the faithfulness of Christ to invade and intercede in the needs of those around us. That is the reason I want to focus this chapter on faithfulness in the account of Jesus' miracle of healing of the courtier's son (John 4:46-54).

The crowds swirled around the Master. He was back in Cana of Galilee after His visit to Jerusalem, where He had cleansed the temple, driving out the money changers. News of that had traveled far and wide. His new fame, the mighty acts He performed, and His transformation of water into wine a short time before made Him the man of the hour. He received a hero's welcome.

The people surrounded Him with buzzing excitement. They pressed in upon Him with provincial enthusiasm for one of their own countrymen who had become the talk of Israel. Local pride brought people flocking to Him. What would He do next? What sign or wonder would astound them further?

We look into Jesus' face and see...sadness. The faithless people wanted more signs and not the word He wanted to give about God's love and the kingdom. He looked at the people, longing to touch the deeper need in them with the miracle of God's faithfulness. But they did not recognize either who He really was or what miracle He could perform in their souls.

The Lord, responding to authentic human need, greeted him tenderly and asked him to speak.

Then suddenly, a wave of amazement rippled over the crowd. A royal official in high standing in Herod's court had entered the edge of the crowd. He had traveled the 20 miles from Capernaum to see Jesus.

The crowd parted with solicitous deference, making a passage corridor for the courtier to come face-to-face with Jesus. The Master turned his attention from the crowd to meet the man.

It was obvious that the otherwise contained and sufficient official was distraught. Nothing could stop him. Single-minded determination pressed him through the crowd. The Lord, responding to authentic human need, greeted him tenderly and asked him to speak.

With urgency mingled with pathos, the man sobbed and told his plight, "My son is at the point of death with a burning fever. News of your mighty acts has reached us at Capernaum. Come down and heal my son!"

The crowd around Jesus responded with expectancy. Surely the Lord would go with him immediately in order to heal the boy. One more sign and wonder for the thrill-hungry but faithless crowd.

Again, a sadness descended over Jesus' face. He looked away from the courtier to the frenzied people cheering for a new miracle. "Unless you see signs and wonders you will not believe," he said firmly, pointedly (John 4:48 rsv). The word was spoken to the crowd, not to the nobleman, for the word forms are plural.

The anguished, worried parent was persistent. His mind was on nothing but his son who was dying. "Sir, come down before my child dies!" he cried out pathetically and urgently (John 4:49).

The Master turned again to him. His face brightened. His countenance was radiant, and His voice was filled with divine authority. "Go; your son will live" (4:50 rsv). The air was filled with hope. The courtier looked into Jesus' eyes, and as he gazed, something happened inside of him. Faith was born. Trust in the Master's words flowed with surging power in his soul. The longer he looked into Jesus' face, the more confident he became. A peace flushed over him, and he realized his son was well. In the presence of the Lord, he knew that his request had been answered. Joy leaped up inside of him. He could not wait to get back to Capernaum to see for himself and hold his healed son in his arms.

⤖ ⬥ ⬦ ⤛

There are few verses in Scripture more beautiful and filled with faithfulness than John's account of the official's response. "The man believed the word that Jesus spoke to him, and he went his way" (4:50). A song of hope and assurance rang in his heart. His son was going to live. The refrain lingered through the journey.

As the courtier neared his home, he was met by his servants. He could tell at a distance that his fondest wish was true. When they blurted out the triumphant good news that his son was well, he was not surprised. With excitement, he inquired the hour when the fever had subsided. The same faith he had felt when he looked into the face of Jesus pulsed in his being when the servants said, "Yesterday at the seventh hour the fever left him" (John 4:52). One o'clock in the afternoon. A thoughtful, far away look came over his face. He was thinking about the Master. The very hour Jesus had spoken the word that his son would be well, the lad was healed. Gratitude beyond expression filled his heart. And then, an irrepressible desire to see his healed boy!

John has given us a miracle with profound meaning, an incident bursting with implications for us. Each time the apostle recorded one of the miracles, he told us what happened and then pressed us to wonder about the deeper meaning of what can happen to us.

This is the miracle of intercessory prayer. We see the potential of bringing our concerns for people we love to the Master.

The account has several crucial things to say to us about faithfulness in prayer for the sickness, suffering, and supplications of the people of our lives.

This miracle will have its intended impact on us if, as we consider its meaning, each of us focuses on people in need for whom we worry and feel deep anxiety. Most of us have loved ones in our families, among our friends, and in our circle of influence who weigh heavily on our hearts. How shall we pray? Does prayer make any difference? If God knows about their needs, how will our fleeting intercession make any difference?

Faithfulness in Action

The first thing this delightful account tells us is that the medium is the first part of a miracle. Some years ago, Marshall McLuhan became famous for his advertising phrase, "The medium is the message." In the case of this miracle, the medium of healing between the Master and the child was the expectant, persistent father who would not leave anything unattempted or untried to get to Jesus and present his need. It was in response to his amazing pertinacity that Jesus healed the sick, fevered child.

We are struck with wonder. The account really teaches that there are some things Christ will not do until we ask in faith-filled, intercessory prayer.

Note the progression. The man came to Jesus. Pride and self-sufficiency were cast aside. The man surrendered his need completely. He trusted the Lord unreservedly. And he returned home with confident trust.

That is the quality of faithfulness the Lord wants to develop in courageous, praying Christians today. E. Stanley Jones put it directly:

> Prayer does not pull God to us, it pulls us to God. It aligns our wills with His will, so that He can do things through us that He would not otherwise have been able to do…If God has left certain things open in the universe around us to the contingency of man's will—things which will not be done unless man acts—is it strange that He has left certain things open, contingent upon prayer—things which will never be done unless we do them through prayer?

Intercessory prayer is faithfulness in action, pressing through the crowd to place the need before the Master. It is love and imagination reaching their highest and widest dimensions. And the Lord is always ready to respond. In fact, He has motivated the prayer, and He is more ready to answer than we may be to ask.

The Lord's intense longing to bless seems to be graciously limited by His desire for our intercessory prayers. His love flows freely in response to people who pray for others. Intercessory prayer is one of the highest expressions of love, of a readiness to receive and yield to the working of Christ's mighty power. We are called to be cooperative agents in the accomplishment of the Lord's purposes. And the miracles the Lord wants to perform around us begin within us, giving us the boldness to come to Him about people and their problems and perplexities. Here is the stupendous mystery and the absolute certainty: Christ sometimes waits to act until we pray confident, loving prayers of intercession.

Listen to the Master as He gives us our royal and holy calling. "If you abide in me, and my words abide in you, ask whatever you will, and it shall be done for you" (John 15:7). "But wait," we say, "that kind of faith is beyond me." No easy escape. The Lord says, "If you have faith as a grain of mustard seed, you will say to this mountain, 'Move from here to there,' and it will move; and nothing will be impossible to you" (Matthew 17:20-21 rsv). The words engender faith. We want to dare to be the medium of the miracle.

—+—⊫✦⊰—+—

And yet, a question lingers...and then rumbles: Why, knowing the promises of power in response to intercessory prayer, do we pray so furtively and faithlessly—if at all? Perhaps the reason is that we have never grappled with the law of the universe that intercessory prayers are an essential part of the unleashing of the faithfulness of our Lord. Or perhaps we believe in the power of evil more than the power of Christ's Spirit. We fear being totally discouraged if we pray and things do not work out as we had hoped. So we pray seldom, expect little, and are rewarded with even less.

Jesus Christ came to tell us that God loves to bless His people. "It is your Father's good pleasure to give you the kingdom," He said (Luke 12:32). But the kingdom is His rule and authority. Intercessory prayer is seeking and surrendering to the will of God in the life of a person. The miracle in us as the medium of prayer power is total relinquishment. Christ knows what is best for the people we love.

Long before He performed the miracle in the courtier's son at one o'clock that afternoon, the miracle of faith had been engendered in the boy's father. That challenges us to precede our intercessory prayers by taking prolonged time in prayer with the Lord. Seek Him before you seek the answer to the prayer of intercession. Abide in His presence. Allow Him to abide in you. Ask for the gift of faith and the knowledge of how to pray. The miracle will begin with you! The fruit of faithfulness will grow.

The Release of God's Resources

The second thing this exciting account of the healing of the nobleman's son communicates is that there is no distance in the power of faithful prayer. Jesus did not have to go to the fevered lad to heal him. This was a portent and prelude to His ubiquitous, omnipresent ministry as the ascended Lord, and of imputed faithfulness in us.

This tells us several things. Only once did Jesus call His mighty acts miracles. He consistently referred to them as the works of God.

> Truly, truly, I say to you, the Son can do nothing of his own accord, but only what he sees the Father doing…The works which the Father has granted me to accomplish, these very works which I am doing, bear me witness that the Father has sent me (John 5:19,36 rsv).

Later in His ministry, Jesus again underlined the fact that what He did was a result of the unlimited power of God in Him. On the night before He was crucified, He said,

> Do you not believe that I am in the Father and the Father in Me? The words that I speak to you I do not speak on My own authority; but the Father who dwells in Me does the works (John 14:10).

The amazing resources of God were released through Him. He did not have to be physically present at the healing of the nobleman's son because it was the omnipresent power of God that was released at His command.

The same is true today. The name of Jesus releases the same power that healed the lad. "Truly, truly, I say to you, he who believes in me will also do the works that I do; and greater works than these will he do, because I go to the Father" (John 14:12 RSV). The promise for our prayers becomes very exciting. "Whatever you ask in my name, I will do it" (John 14:13 RSV).

And that is true for you and me for our intercessions today. Christ is alive. "In that day you will know that I am in my Father, and you in me, and I in you" (John 14:20 RSV). What that means is that we will be guided on how to pray and then be enabled to pray with assurance for others. The same power exposed in the Messiah will flow through our prayers to other people.

Distance makes no difference for the prayer of faithfulness. Neither geographical nor psychological distance is of any consequence. Often, we are separated from people we love: Some live at great distances, and others with whom we are present are castled in the citadels of their own aloneness, which is difficult to penetrate. But we can pray and know that Christ is at work. We can participate with Him in the release of His amazing resources if we will pray.

I want to suggest a new word for our faithfulness: *Christo-telepathy.* It is a combination of *telepathy* and *Christ. Telepathy* is the communication of one mind with another at a distance by other than sensory means—contact beyond the physical senses of sight, touch, and hearing of proximity. *Tele* means "distance." *Pathy* is from the root of the Greek *pathein,* "passion," meaning to suffer or feel deeply for, or on behalf of another. *Sympathy* and *empathy* come from this stem. *Christopathy,* on the other hand, is spiritual emotion aroused by meditation in prayer. We feel Christ's love, passion, and suffering concern. A *Christotelepathy,* then, is the experience of the love of Christ engendered by Him for another person at a distance. We can reach the needs of others by communication with Christ, who is more passionately concerned than we are.

Evelyn Underhill, the great Christian mystic, once said that through power and love, one human spirit can touch another human spirit. It can take the soul and lift it into the atmosphere of Christ. People in need of help will find that the person who prays is a transmitter of the redeeming power of Christ.

We have all had the experience of having a person on our mind, only to discover later that that person thought of us at the same time. Also, we have had times when a concern or alarm stirs within us at the very time another person is in great need, danger, or trouble. This is telepathy, the communication of living souls. Faithfulness in prayer raises this to the level of Christotelepathy, communication with another through the channel of prayer with Christ. There is no limitation of distance. The Lord has ordained intercessory prayer as the release of His miraculous power in the life of another, regardless of where he or she is, near or far.

Concern for another person is a message from Christ that He's ready to work in that person's life if we will cooperate with intercessory prayer. The person's prayers for himself or herself are not enough. Christ made it that way. He is the initiator of our desire to pray because He wants to reproduce His love in us for the person.

Assurance from Faithfulness

Authentic intercession is rewarded by the "Go your way, your son lives" kind of assurance that Jesus gave to the courtier. That takes relinquishment. We are to pray once and thank Christ repeatedly that He has heard and that He will answer according to His will and the ultimate good of the person for whom we have prayed. It is also a gift of Christ to "go our way," leaving in His hands the matter we have prayed about earnestly. To continue to worry after we have interceded is a sure sign that we have not surrendered the need and are still carrying it ourselves for another person. This is lack of faith that the Lord has heard and is active to answer the concern He has placed on our hearts. That's why we need the fruit of faithfulness.

Paul was nourished by the fruit of faithfulness in his intercessory prayers for the Ephesians. In chapter 1 he tells his beloved friends how and what he is praying for them:

[I] do not cease to give thanks for you, making mention of you in my prayers: that the God of our Lord Jesus Christ, the Father of glory, may give to you the spirit of wisdom and revelation in the knowledge of Him, the eyes of your understanding being enlightened; that you may know what is the hope of His calling, what are the riches of the glory of His inheritance in the saints, and what is the exceeding greatness of His power toward us who believe, according to the working of His mighty power which He worked in Christ when He raised Him from the dead and seated Him at His right hand in the heavenly places (Ephesians 1:16-20).

This is a mighty charter for our expression of the character trait of faithfulness in our prayers for others. It gives us a progression for these prayers.

1. *Thanksgiving.* Profound gratitude for the privilege of intercessory prayer and for the fruit of faithfulness to persist in the opening of the floodgate for the flow of the Lord's blessing in the life of the person for whom we pray.

2. Next pray for *the person's relationship with the Lord.* Our essential prayer is that people come to know Christ as Savior, Lord, and indwelling power. If a person does not know the Lord, prayer must focus on the urgent supplication that whatever he or she is going through will bring him or her to complete trust in the Lord. So often we pray for solutions before salvation. It may be that people have been checkmated in some difficult situation so they may discover the Lord's love and power.

3. Now pray for *wisdom.* Wisdom is a very special gift given to people who are in need that they will have supernatural discernment and insight to know what is the Lord's best for their lives.

4. Pray for *power.* People need strength to act on what the Lord guides as a result of our prayers for them. When we intercede for them supernatural power from Christ's Spirit will be given.

5. Pray for *love.* The eyes of a person's heart need to be enlightened to see that they belong to the Lord, that fear of death is past, that the future is in His hands, and that He is working His purposes out. Pray for the rebirth of hope!

6. The last element of praying for another is *telling him or her.* Call, write, communicate that you are interceding daily. That may present the opportunity to talk further about the Lord and His amazing resources.

Now with the special gift of imagination, picture yourself approaching the crowd around Jesus as the courtier did. You long to get through to Him about someone you love. See the crowd part and the open corridor directly to the Lord made for you. He is there for you. Now stand before Him face-to-face, heart-to-heart. He is waiting for you to ask for what He is ready to give. Tell Him about a person or persons on your heart. Then wait for His answer. *At this very moment you prayed,* says Jesus, *My power has been released in the person for* whom you interceded. My will shall be done, in My timing, according to My plan, and for the now and forever blessing of your loved one. You and I are of one heart now. We both love and care. Now go your way in faithfulness.

19

Within You to Give You the Power of Gentleness

Meekness is not weakness.
It is power under Christ's control.

There is a stereotype for gentleness in our culture that is anything but attractive. It is a milquetoast kind of person whose only vocal contribution is the sound of the throat being cleared for speech that never comes.

If you have bought this stereotype, it may come as a distinct shock to you to know that meekness or gentleness is a characteristic of Christ that He can implant and wants to develop in you. Christ wants to make us His meek and gentle people who can display His power.

In Paul's inventory of the fruit of the Spirit, the King James Version translates this quality as "meekness," but it means something quite different from the weakness often associated with the word. *Gentleness,* as it is translated in the New King James Version, is a far better word.

Authentic Gentleness

Authentic gentleness is one of the most miraculous manifestations of the inner power of Christ's indwelling. It requires absolute trust in His ongoing work in others. It responds to the wonder of what people have been through, not to what they have done. It addresses the emerging child, often hurt and battered, in other people.

The Lord is consistently gentle with us. He stands beside us in the midst of trouble and tragedy, nursing us through it all. That is the same kind of encouragement the people around us need.

What does it mean to be gentle in life's tensions and problems? It certainly does not mean simply having a soft, easy lack of concern. Moses was referred to as one of the meekest men in all of Israel, and yet he marshaled the mass exodus of a diverse company of people and brought them through the wilderness to the Promised Land.

But it is in Jesus Christ that we see gentleness in its true light. Though the word is not used, the passage which shows us true gentleness is the account of the Passover feast in the thirteenth chapter of John's Gospel.

> Jesus, knowing that the Father had given all things into His hands, and that He had come from God and was going to God, rose from supper and laid aside His garments, took a towel and girded Himself. After that, He poured water into a basin and began to wash the disciples' feet (John 13:3-5).

Jesus knew who He was and what He had come to do. He could do the servant's work. His life and death portray gentleness. He loved His enemies and followers alike, those who deceived Him, betrayed Him, and crucified Him. He was totally free of defensiveness. The same character that was in Christ can be in us.

When we are truly meek...we know we are loved and are therefore free to be the unique, special, transformed people we were meant to be.

The word *gentleness—praotēs,* from *praus* in Greek—has a profound implication for us. For Aristotle, it stood for the mean point between too much anger and too little anger, a point between overexpression and underexpression. A meek or gentle person was one who was under such control that he or she was able to express the reality of each emotion without excess.

There is more. The word *praus* describes an animal which has been brought under the reins or control of a master and is now guidable. The truly meek are those who have gone through an experience when their arrogant self-will has been broken. They have come to a place of deep humility. *Praus* in Greek is the opposite of *huperēphania*—pride—which is always contrasted with humility. *Huperēphania* is holding oneself above others instead of caring for others guided by the control of the Master's reins.

When we are truly meek, we know who we are because we know to Whom we belong. We do not have to be defensive or justify ourselves any longer. We know we are loved and are therefore free to love and free to be the unique, special, transformed people we were meant to be. Once the defensive pride is taken from us by an authentic experience of humility, we are able to treat others as Christ has treated us.

⊷ ⋙⊹⋘ ⊶

I was fascinated as I studied the word *gentleness* in many different biblical settings and found it to be a relational word. It deals with the correction of one Christian by another and how to treat persons in the midst of problems.

After Paul has listed the fruit or characteristics of the Spirit to the Galatians, in the sixth chapter he says: "Brethren, if a man is overtaken in any trespass, you who are spiritual restore such a one in a spirit of gentleness, considering yourself lest you also be tempted" (6:1). It is out of a recognition of our own inadequacy that we can be tender toward others.

I read an old newspaper account of a speech reportedly given by the outspoken atheist Madalyn Murray O'Hair. Her audience of young people listened patiently as she gave her speech opposing religion in American life and her deprecation of God and faith. When she concluded, a young woman stood up and spoke with gentle purpose. She thanked Ms. O'Hair for coming to speak and told her that the young people had listened with attention. Then she thanked her for showing them what an atheist really is, and she expressed gratitude to her for strengthening their beliefs by her attack. Then she told her how sorry they were for her. Again she thanked her for coming and said they now had even more love and faith in God as a result of seeing what life without God would be.

There is a meekness in defense of the faith! Meekness that has strength. In the deafening applause that followed the girl's words, Ms. O'Hair left the platform.

The Secret of Blessedness

Meekness should be the basis of receiving the word of God. James says, "Lay aside all filthiness and overflow of wickedness, and receive with meekness the implanted word, which is able to save your souls" (James 1:21).

James has given us the secret in the word *receive*. True meekness or gentleness is receptivity. We cannot give away what we have not received. Nor can we receive all that God wants to give us unless we give away what is given to us for others. This is the magnificent meaning of the third beatitude.

The gentle inherit the earth. They are the blessed. Note the progression in the beatitude. Blessed means beloved, belonging to God, cherished, called, and chosen. Those who know their sublime status are able to be gentle, completely open to what God wants to give, and sensitive to His guidance. Because they are, they can inherit the earth. The phrase has its roots in Psalm 37:11: "The meek shall inherit the earth and shall delight themselves in the abundance of peace."

To the Hebrews, it meant first the Promised Land, then the providence of God, and finally the fulfillment of the messianic age. Surely the latter was on Jesus' mind when He affirmed meekness as an essential secret of blessedness. All that He had come to be and do would be available to those who were receptive. His nature would be implanted and His power unleashed in them.

Paul underlined this when he called us "joint heirs with Christ" (Romans 8:17). Our inheritance was sealed on Calvary, assured on Easter, and completed on Pentecost. Meekness is being open to the new and fresh thing the Lord wants to give so that we can become riverbeds for the flow of His grace to others.

Now look at the results of gentleness in Psalm 37:11. Catch the power and significance if you will. The meek shall eat and be satisfied. The Lord will guide the meek to abundant peace. He will teach them His way.

We inherit the earth because we are children of the Father,

and everything that is His belongs to us. We are joint heirs with Christ. When His nature is in us, we become free to be gentle, free to love because His love has healed our personalities. We know we are God's children and are free to be that with abandonment.

> Behold what manner of love the Father has bestowed on us, that we should be called children of God!...Beloved, now we are children of God; and it has not yet been revealed what we shall be, but we know that when He is revealed, we shall be like Him, for we shall see Him as He is (1 John 3:1-2).

Far from being apologetic in manner, Christ's gentleness that we inherit is a mind-set that shapes and tempers the style of what we are as Christians. Now on the basis of all that, we can allow the Lord to cure our future worries; activate the characteristic of gentleness implicit in our new heredity; become a gracious receiver. I am convinced that what Christ has done in the past in our lives is nothing in comparison with what He is ready to do. Now. Today. Trust Him.

The only time the future tense is used in a salutation or greeting in the epistles of the New Testament is in the second letter of John. He says: "Grace, mercy, and peace will be with you from God the Father and from the Lord Jesus Christ"

(2 John 3). That's the assurance I need. We are rooted in the very character of Christ, in His plan for us, the way He works with us, and what happens inside us.

Gentleness is also a spiritual muscle inherent in our new nature, waiting to be exercised to unlock the resources of the power of Christ to apply to our specific situations. Only that kind of inner strength is an antidote to anxiety. Only faith can cure our lack of trust. And as the nature of Christ begins to grow in us, we become identifiably gentle people with power.

20

Within You to Give You Victory

Self-mastering is the result of yielding ourselves to the Master.

Do you believe that you are a unique, never-to-be-repeated miracle? To be nobody but the person you were created to be is a battle, and it takes self-control to win it. May the living Christ go in you to give you victory.

Self-control, the final jewel of the inner splendor encompassed in Paul's special term *fruit,* is the one which makes all the rest operative. To the Greek, self-control was to have "power over oneself." Paul grasped this quality from the four cardinal virtues of the Stoics and claimed it as one of the imputed vibrancies of the indwelling Christ. The Greek word, *egkrateia,* means holding control.

This sublime fruit of Christ's Spirit is not negative. It does not consist of a list of what we are against or will not do. Rather, it consists of a very positive capacity to know who we are and what we will do because the Spirit of Christ is in control of our abilities and aptitudes, as well as our appetites. We can have power over ourselves only when we have submitted to Christ's control and power in us. Christ-control is the basis of self-control. It means living with the assurance that Christ is in us. Such an awareness results in the development of the special person each of us was created to be. It is very exciting to realize that our Lord has a strategy and plan for each of us.

We often think of personality only as the irrevocable result of parental and environmental conditioning. A young man said to his father, "What I am is what you've made me." That is to evade the opportunity and responsibility we all have to accept the Lord's reshaping of our personalities. He can affirm and strengthen what we are, in keeping with the uniqueness He has planned for us, and then He can reform anything that distorts or hinders our becoming all that we were meant to be.

When we yield our personalities to the Lord's scrutiny and renovation, He begins a magnificent transformation. That means surrendering our values, attitudes, actions, and reactions to Him. In profound times of prayer and meditation, we can talk to Him about the person we are in every dimension and relationship and then listen to Him as He tenderly shows us areas that need to be remolded to be more like Him.

The Hero in Your Soul

The secret of discovering our truly unique personality is to focus on Christ. We become like our heroes, and He is the only reliable hero of our souls. In 1928, Arthur John Gossip entitled one of his books *The Hero in Thy Soul.* I like that! The better we know Christ, the more we concentrate on His message and life, and the closer we will come to being the special, distinct persons He intended. It is amazing. The deeper we grow in Christ, the more we become free to be our true selves. He does not put us into a straitjacket of sameness. Rather, He liberates us with new values, priorities, attitudes, and goals which begin to surface in our personalities. Human nature can be changed. We do not have to remain the people we are.

A few years ago, I experienced great physical reformation in intensive physiotherapy. In a series of ten sessions with a highly trained physiotherapist, my body underwent remarkable changes. Tightened tendons, conditioned by years of bad habits of posture were stretched and released. A hump in my back, formed by long hours slouched over my writing desk, was removed. Constricted muscles in my stomach that were pulling me down into a stooped posture were liberated so I could stand up straight. Years of unhealthy self-conditioning of my body were reversed. Over the months of therapy, I grew an inch! I did not have to be the physical person I was for the rest of my life. My body was like plastic, and under the skilled hands of the therapist, I was liberated to stand, walk, and sit differently.

I have shared this personal experience as an illustration that none of us needs to remain the person he or she is. What that series of treatments did to my body, Christ has done and continues to do with my personality. I am not the personality I was; nor am I the person I will be. Seldom a day goes by without the Lord's impact.

Ever since I yielded the control of my personality development to Him, He has been at work. He's not finished with me, nor will He ever be. In daily times with Him, He helps me look back over what I have been, said, and done. He always begins with what has been creative and good. Then, with masterful sensitivity, He penetrates into my relationships with myself and others. His questions are incisive: *Why did you feel it necessary to do or say that? What would you have been like if you had been trusting Me and My guidance in that situation?* Following that is a remedial time of thinking with Him on how I can be more His person in the future.

Five *I*'s for Discovering the Real *I*

The Lord offers us five *I*'s for discovering the real *I*. The first is *introspection.* That means daring to look inward to discover the roots of our personality. Why are we the people we are? What shaped our character? Whom are we trying to emulate? What is right and what is less than maximum?

The second step is *integration*. Christ takes inner control over our persons. When we put Him first in our lives, seek first His kingdom, and want what He wants for us, there is a new integration around His lordship. This is the control that liberates. Memories are sorted out, values are scrutinized, hopes are refashioned.

The third flows naturally. From integration comes *integrity*. We can dare to be outwardly what the Lord has enabled us to be inwardly. Integrity is the capacity to act in keeping with our beliefs and convictions—consistency! People around us will be able to say those seven dynamic words we all long to hear: "What you see is what you get." We all want to be people on whom others can depend in life's changes and challenges. We urgently desire to be the kind of parents, friends, and leaders whose attitudes and actions will be predictably consistent with the individual persons we really are.

Intuition is the fourth dimension. A life under Christ's control is gifted with an inner device that discerns what's right and does it. Gifts of wisdom and discernment give us X-ray vision. They help us to see beneath the surface of things. We are empowered to think clearly and feel sensitively about what is going on around us. Our minds and emotions become agents of the Spirit to guide us in times of pressure and opportunity.

I have a friend who has yielded to Christ's control so completely that he can penetrate deeply into problems and see the potential for advancement they offer. People around him are often heard to remark, "That guy sees and understands. How come his perception is so sharp?" The fruit of self-control as a result of Christ control is the only explanation. His faithfulness to daily prayer makes him an effective, intuitive leader. It is a supernatural gift. Without the indwelling Christ, he would be as dull, insensitive, and unadventuresome as the people he constantly amazes.

The final *I* is *individuality*. We hear a lot of "I've got to be me!" individualism which is a poor facsimile for Christ-centered individuality. Individualism is a self-conscious effort to be different and distinct. It always calls attention to itself and must be fortified by disclaimers such as "Well, that's who I am. If you don't like it, that's your problem!" Individuality grows inadvertently when the focus is on Christ and not on ourselves. We do not need to strive to be different. Christ is our difference. He makes us individuals who are free to live by grace and follow His guidance. The result will be people unlike anyone else, yet people who are concerned more about others than themselves.

The old statement "God threw away the mold after He made him" is both true and untrue. Our mold is Christ and we come back to Him repeatedly for the clay of our personalities to be recast. The result will be freedom from self-consciousness or defensiveness.

In the context of all this, we can take another look at the word self-control as a translation of *egkrateia*. A Christ-controlled person has gone through the refining process. He or she has been hammered out on the anvil of the Lord's gracious, but persistent, reshaping. There is freedom from eccentric extremes and indulgences. The things which do not contribute to the Lord's best for us can be discarded or used without compulsion. Nothing that we eat or drink will be needed to fortify a depleted ego. Behavior patterns which trip us up in following Christ can be faced and surrendered to Him. All the things we consume or the distracting habits we form out of intemperance will be dislodged from their hold on us.

Balance in a Beguiling World

There is a great word called *equipoise*. It means balance. When the inner power of Christ is balanced perfectly with the outward pressures of the world, that is equipoise. It is another way of describing self-control.

We live in such a beguiling world. As we are pulled in so many directions it is easy to allow our minds to drift into fantasies, our wills to make decisions inconsistent with the character of Christ, and our bodies to be engaged in practices which are not in keeping with His lordship.

Everything that was manifest in the character of Jesus of Nazareth is reproducible in you and me. "The Father and I will come and make our home in you," Christ said (my paraphrase of John 14:23). It is a word of cheer and a word of challenge.

Paul gives the Galatians, and us, the secret of how to realize power over oneself. He says that we have crucified the flesh, and now as we live by the Spirit we should also walk by the Spirit: "The Spirit has given us life; he must also control our lives" (Galatians 5:25 GNT).

When we are fully in touch with who we are—the new person we are in Christ— an unmistakable outward radiance will reflect the splendor within... There is no way to hide it.

The term *flesh* is a kind of biblical shorthand for our humanity independent and separate from Jesus Christ. The exciting life begins when our minds, emotions, wills, and bodies are joyously surrendered to Christ's infinite control. That also includes every relationship of our lives.

Do you remember when you took your first steps "in Christ"? Just as we learn to commit our weight to the ground step by step, in the same way we reach out to venture love and peace, patience and kindness—beyond our own hoarded resources, confident of Christ's limitless and ever-ready supply. Soon we will have acquired one of the greatest skills of all: self-control.

For Christians battling the pull of the lower nature, Paul's special term *fruit* is an invitation to a radical transformation of the whole of human existence. Paul lists the "works of the flesh" in Galatians 5 and heralds the fruit of the Spirit as the antidote. For example, when we go around nursing giant-size hostilities, initiating quarrels, and constantly putting up opposite points of view, we are boycotting the Spirit's stores of gentleness and peace.

When we are fully in touch with who we are—the new person we are in Christ—an unmistakable outward radiance will reflect the splendor within. We have discovered the control within that opens the channel to becoming the new breed of men and women we were intended to be. There is no way to hide it.

I'll never forget a wonderful period of uninterrupted time I had with my mother a few years before she died. Mother had sewn a new red dress for the occasion, spent the morning at the hairdresser, cleaned the house, had the coffee on the stove, and was all ready for my arrival.

We sat and talked like we had not talked for years, and like we might never talk again. She got out some of the old scrapbooks and albums, and entrusted to me a photo that is now one of my most cherished possessions. It was a picture of my father when he was my age. Years before she had put it away to give to me in such a moment. My eyes devoured the photo for marks of the heredity we shared. I traced the lines and contours in my father's face now evident in my own.

I trust the same kind of excitement has been in you as you have read these chapters. And now I just have to ask: Do you see the inescapable marks of an emerging family likeness as a joint heir with Christ of your heavenly Father? Are you thrilled by the true delight of being able to express the graces and characteristics of Christ in your daily life and relationships? Awesome, isn't it? He wants to make you more like Himself!

Is it happening? Are we giving the world a symmetrical, authentic, fully formed image of Christ? There is still time. Spiritual growth is not a matter of chronology alone. It's a matter of your spirit. Of heart. Of who you are to the next person you meet. In the next crisis you face. In the next moment you live.

So, once more I give my blessing to you:

May the omnipotent, omniscient, omnipresent Christ go with you: before you to show the way, behind you to protect you, beside you to befriend you, above you to watch over you, and within you to enable you to live life to the fullest.

Five Gifts

Christ's love for us reaches deep and far
and He has many gifts to give.
Five of these gifts, if accepted by us,
will help us in how we live.

The first gift that He does give
is to prepare the way for me.
He goes before to open the hearts
of the people He wants me to see.

He also stands behind me.
He protects me from the rear.
Where trouble is often brewing,
with Him I will not fear.

He holds my hand and walks by my side,
and never will let me go.
Whether I'm on the top of a mountain
or down and feeling low.

For He always will watch over me,
I know that in my heart.
His plan for my life is perfect
and from me He'll never part.

To have Him indwell my heart and soul
is His greatest gift to me.
He gives me His love, peace, and joy
so I can relax and just be free.

I thank you, Christ, for these five gifts—
special they are, each hour.
I am a protected disciple of Yours
and led each day by Your Power.[4]

By my friend Sue McCollum,
written in response to hearing my benediction.

Notes

1. A.T. Robertson, *Word Pictures in the New Testament,* vol. 5 (Nashville, TN: Broadman Press, 1943), p. 249.

2. James S. Stewart, *The Gates of New Life* (Edinburgh: T. and T. Clark, 1937, paperback ed. 1976), pp. 90-91.

3. Amy Carmichael, *Edges of His Way* (Fort Washington, PA: Christian Literature Crusade, 1975), p. 100.

4. Sue McCollum, "Five Gifts" © 2005 Sue McCollum. Used by permission.

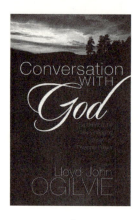

Conversation with God

*Experience the Life-Changing
Impact of Personal Prayer*

Lloyd John Ogilvie

What if Praying Were Like Talking with a Friend?

Prayer can truly be like that…and more, says bestselling author Lloyd John Ogilvie. In this book he draws on years of experiencing God as a friend to paint a fresh picture of prayer—an approach that is as much listening as speaking, and that leaves you feeling understood, appreciated, and invigorated.

Clearly and simply, he explains the many dimensions of prayer with chapter topics like…

- God Begins the Conversation
- The Conversation Deepens
- Conversation About Guidance

And uniquely, he then provides a 30-day guide to help you put into practice what you're learning.

As you begin to enjoy give-and-take conversation with God as a part of everyday life, you'll experience the truth that He is always available…so you never need to feel alone or isolated. And you'll find prayer to be more refreshing, profound, and meaningful than you may ever have imagined possible.

Excellent for group discussions or as a personal guide.

To read a sample chapter, go to
www.harvesthousepublishers.com

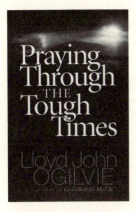

Praying Through the Tough Times
Lloyd John Ogilvie

*"Lord, I can't carry the burdens
myself any longer."*

Perhaps you feel empty...discon-
nected...worn down by the difficulties
of life and relationships. God seems
distant. You find it difficult to pray.

Longtime pastor and bestselling
author Lloyd John Ogilvie understands the tough times from
his own experience. In this book of 100 prayers—blended with
Scripture verses and encouraging thoughts—he gently but chal-
lengingly offers words when your own words fail. Here are ways
to ask the Lord to clear your vision so you can...

- see the tough situations in light of His solutions
- see the difficult people you love through His eyes
- see an uncertain future transformed when you place
  it in His hands

As these prayers help you reconnect with the God who cares
about you and wants to comfort you, He will guide you from
panic to His perspective...and then to peace.

*"Dear God, You fill me with a living hope
that no trouble can destroy, no fear can disturb.
Make me a communicator of Your hope.
Hope through me, God of hope!"*

To read a sample chapter, go to
www.harvesthousepublishers.com

More Harvest House Books
by Lloyd John Ogilvie

THE ESSENCE OF HIS PRESENCE

Longtime pastor Lloyd John Ogilvie comes alongside to strengthen you with five assurances of God's loving, always-loyal presence with you and within you. He affirms that God will…

- *go before you to show you the way*
- *go behind you to protect you*
- *go beside you to befriend you*
- *go above you to watch over you*
- *go within you to give you all He knows you need*

GOD'S BEST FOR MY LIFE

Better than your fondest hopes and expectations, God wants to give you His best for your life. This classic bestseller offers 365 devotions that invite you to discover, explore, and enjoy your loving Father each day.

QUIET MOMENTS WITH GOD

These daily prayers will help you nurture a special intimacy with God. You will experience God's blessed assurance as you are comforted by His boundless love and His promises to provide guidance and give strength.

THE RED EMBER IN THE WHITE ASH

Do you sometimes feel tired…burnt out…fearful to engage life? Dr. Ogilvie draws on Scripture to point you to the living and active Holy Spirit. As you see the darkness of fear and discouragement driven out by His flame of godly enthusiasm, you will experience hope and be able to love others with God's love.

To see sample chapters of these books, visit
www.harvesthousepublishers.com